Remembering Cesar
The Legacy of Cesar Chavez

Remembering Cesar
The Legacy of Cesar Chavez

Compiled by Ann McGregor

Edited by Cindy Wathen

Photographs by George Elfie Ballis

Quill Driver Books

Clovis, California

Published by
Quill Driver Books/Word Dancer Press, Inc.
8386 North Madsen Avenue • Clovis, California 93611
559-322-5917 / 800-497-4909 / FAX 559-322-5967

Quill Driver Books' titles may be purchased in quantity at special discounts for educational, fund-raising, business, or promotional use. Please contact Special Markets, Quill Driver Books/Word Dancer Press, Inc. at the above address or phone numbers.

Quill Driver Books project cadre: David Marion, Stephen Blake Mettee, Marilyn Riddle Harper, Linda Kay Weber

ISBN 1-884956-11-4

To order another copy of this book,
please call 1-800-497-4909

First Printing September 2000 • Printed in the United States of America

To Helen Fabela Chavez with profound respect and admiration
and
In memory of Peter Gines Velasco and Mike Vasquez

Library of Congress Cataloging-in-Publication Data

Remembering Cesar Chavez / compiled by Ann McGregor ; edited by Cindy Wathen ;
photographs by George Elfie Ballis.
     p. cm.
   ISBN 1-884956-11-4
     1. Chavez, Cesar, 1927---Pictorial works. 2. Labor leaders--United
States--Biography--Pictorial works. 3. Mexican Americans--Biography--Pictorial works.
4. Mexican American agricultural laborers--History--Sources. 5. Mexican American
agricultural laborers--Pictorial works. 6. Strikes and lockouts--Agricultural
laborers--United States--History--Sources. 7. Strikes and lockouts--Agricultural
laborers--United States--Pictorial works. 8. United Farm Workers--History--Sources. I.
McGregor, Ann, 1920- II. Wathen, Cindy. III. Ballis, George Elfie.

HD6509.C48 R46 2000
331.88'13'092--dc21
[B]
                                                                              00-055379

Contents

Essays

Prayer for the Farmworkers' Struggle

Show me the suffering of the most miserable;
So I will know my people's plight.

Free me to pray for others;
For you are present in every person.

Help me to take responsibility for my own life;
So that I can be free at last.

Give me honesty and patience;
So that I can work with other workers.

Bring forth song and celebration;
So that the Spirit will be alive among us.

Let the Spirit flourish and grow;
So that we will never tire of the struggle.

Let us remember those who have died for justice;
For they have given us life.

Help us love even those who hate us;
So we can change the world.

Amen.

— Cesar Chavez

Preface

To the world, Cesar Chavez will always be known as the labor leader who organized California farmworkers into a union during the twentieth century. He will be remembered for his commitment to nonviolence.

To the thousands living today who knew him, Cesar was not only founder and president of the United Farm Workers of America, AFL-CIO, he was much more. Visionary, crusader, organizer, administrator, teacher, entrepreneur, rebel, hero, father and friend are some of the titles he earned during a lifetime of tireless work and self-sacrifice on behalf of those most exploited of all human beings, farmworkers.

It is intended that this book honor the memory of this authentic American genius and present him to future generations as those of us who knew Cesar Chavez saw him.

Ann McGregor

I never met Cesar Chavez. I was never a volunteer, a farmworker, or even an acquaintance. I never walked a picket line, fasted or marched the state of California. But I know Cesar. I know him through the eyes of his admirers.

Having been born well past the initial grape strikes, I didn't understand who Cesar was until long after he passed away. In assembling this book, I have heard the words of the people who loved him most. I've read their stories and felt their plight. I've marveled at their resolve and handed them my admiration. How else do you a know a man than through his acts?

Every essay included in this book is an act of volunteerism. No contributor has been financially compensated for his or her words. Like Cesar, each found the time to give to a greater good—that of the memory of Cesar and his words. These essays will give you the essence of the man. If you wish to know Cesar, this is where to start.

Cindy Wathen

When Eisenhower went to the White House in January, 1953, I moved into the San Joaquin Valley to edit the *Valley Labor Citizen*, an AFL-CIO weekly.

I quickly realized the two most important California issues:

1. Water—its crucial political, environmental, social and economic implications;

2. Farmworkers—the cold exploitation of workers producing food in the world's richest agricultural empire.

I immersed my passion for justice into both issues.

I set out with my cameras to expose to the world the horrible farmworker conditions in California. In my cherryness, I assumed that once the exposure was done, improvements would naturally follow. (This naiveté was unfounded because I knew of Dorothea Lange's dust bowl photos which shocked, but did not move the country.)

Quickly, my photographic agenda was transformed by my engagement with my subjects. I flipped from being an exposé photographer to becoming a friend, an advocate, a compañero. I was honored to be accepted into their lives with my cameras.

I discovered, contrary to my preconceptions, that my new friends were not to be pitied or patronized for their poverty. They were to be celebrated for the dignity, courage, strength and fortitude they mustered in the face of a grinding, relentless oppression. They became my "clients." My purpose was to use my photos to reflect back to them their dignity and strength—so they could step beyond society's bias and empower themselves to demand from the rest of us their rightful share of the collective wealth they helped to create.

When *La Huelga*—Spanish for "The Strike"—blossomed in 1965, I was immersed in the farm labor community as photographer, researcher and organizer. Chavez quickly emerged as the point man. His magic was amplification. He could take a small incident and transform it into a grand cause. He did this with the small, uneducated life he was given. He did it with the UFW. He did it with the lives of those who joined the cause—*La Causa*. His energy amplified their importance from downtrodden laborers to a large family of valued humanity providing food for America.

That's why, for me, the most significant impressions of Chavez are not photos idealizing the man, but photos which reveal the impact of his amplifications. He might not even be seen in the picture.

In this light, the essential photo of *La Huelga* is the march photo on the cover. The other photos we chose for this book show Chavez's amplification magic.

Most of the photos are undated because they are timeless. They could have been made yesterday or fifty years ago.

George Elfie Ballis

INTRODUCTION

Since his death in 1993, my father has been afforded many honors in communities across California and the nation. Schools, streets, parks and other public places have been named after him. Ironically, these were the kinds of honors he largely eschewed during his lifetime.

Yet, by the strictly material standards some people use to judge success at the end of the twentieth century, Cesar Chavez was not very successful. He never attended high school—although he was very well-read later in life, his formal education ended after the eighth grade. He never owned a house. He didn't own a car. He never made more than $6,000 a year.

"True wealth is not measured in money or status or power," he said in the eulogy for a slain farmworker striker in 1979." It is measured in the legacy we leave behind for those we love and those we inspire." Part of my dad's patrimony, the legacy he left behind, was a powerful conviction that ordinary people could do extraordinary things with the right kind of encouragement and respect.

Although he welcomed the selfless sacrifices of many nonfarmworkers who served over the years on the United Farm Workers staff, he also constantly pushed farmworkers to become the negotiators, administrators, attorneys, accountants and other professionals on whom the UFW came to depend.

One example stands out in my memory. By the mid-and late-1970s, after the union had become established—having won elections and contracts with growers under California's farm labor law that my father pioneered—he set up a special school to train negotiators at La Paz, the UFW's Keene, California, headquarters in the Tehachapi Mountains.

The union invested substantial resources in that school. It offered a comprehensive curriculum of academic subjects and language training, with instruction often supplied by lawyers, economists and other veteran labor experts in collective bargaining.

Many in the UFW wanted to fill the coveted slots in that school with union staff who were college graduates. These folks argued the conventional wisdom that a college education provided the requisite skills to handle the complexities of contract negotiations.

Not my father. He insisted on offering positions in the first negotiating school class to farmworker kids. Many of them had grown up in the movement during the 1960s and 1970s. They too worked for the union, but in those days they were mostly janitors or trash collectors or apprentices in the print shop.

This sparked a big internal fight within the UFW. In the end, my father prevailed, as he usually did. The first class of graduates included a number of young people from farmworker backgrounds few would have considered material for union negotiators.

Soon most of the graduates were going toe-to-toe with the toughest growers and attorneys agribusiness had to offer. And they performed well. Some are still with the UFW. Others went on to successful careers outside the union.

But to this day, all credit their success to the faith one small, brown-skinned man had in the ability of ordinary people to do extraordinary things.

I should know. I'm one of them. In 1977, I was an apprentice in the union's print shop at La Paz.

Today, I head the National Farm Workers Service Center, Inc., a nonprofit organization related to the UFW founded by my father in the 1960s. It now operates a popular network of Spanish-language radio stations featuring news and Mexican music. It also constructs and manages affordable, high-quality rental housing for low and very low income farmworkers and Latinos.

Mine is but one memory of my father. Hundreds of people have shared similar stories with me. Now Ann McGregor—who worked with my dad for years—and Cindy Wathen have collected many of these stories in this book.

These rememberances provide glimpses through the eyes of others into the character and qualities of a man who helped thousands of farmworkers improve their own lives and taught important lessons about justice and self-sacrifice to millions of people who never worked on a farm.

Paul F. Chavez

"All my life, I have been driven by one dream, one goal, one vision: to overthrow a farm labor system in this nation which treats farmworkers as if they were not important human beings. Farmworkers are not agricultural implements. They are not beasts of burden to be used and discarded."

— Cesar Chavez

My feet are sore,
my spirit intense.

For the migrant farmworker, each day was endless; each night he was exhausted and often hungry. His life stood in stunning contrast to the comfortable lives of families who savored the fruits of his labor. In a land that promised plenty, migrant farmworkers in the 1960s had no voice, no rights, and no protection. Cesar Chavez knew their troubles firsthand. Once a migrant farmworker, he was small, soft-spoken, and low-key, a guy you could easily lose in a crowd. But this gentle giant woke up the drowsy conscience of the most powerful country in the world.

For years, Americans had brought home sweet, plump clusters of table grapes without a second thought. By the late 1960s, Caesar Chavez had turned the decision of whether or not to buy grapes into a powerful political act. This quiet man with dark, Indian features had changed the ordinary act of buying groceries into an opportunity to help others by exercising the power of socially responsible buying habits.

Farmworkers had been trying to organize a union for more than one hundred years. In 1965, they began a bitter five-year strike against grape growers around Delano, California. Two and one-half years later, in the hungry winter of 1968 with no resolution in sight, they were tired and frustrated.

Cesar had already decided to ask for help. He believed that if people in communities throughout the nation knew about the needless suffering of farmworkers, they would rise to the occasion and do what they could to help. Taking a bold leap of faith, Cesar invited consumers to join in solidarity with his United Farm Workers (UFW). He asked them to send a message to the grape growers by boycotting California table grapes. The boycott began slowly, but built steadily over the next couple of years. First California, then the rest of the nation and even Canada, joined in support of the strikers.

In the meantime, some of the strikers had become impatient. Among some of them, particularly some of the young men, there began the murmurs of violence; some wanted to strike back at those who had abused them and their families. By fighting back, they thought they could prove their machismo, their manliness. But Cesar rejected that part of our culture "that tells young men that you're not a man if you don't fight back." The boycott had followed in the tradition of Cesar's hero, Mahatma Gandhi, whose practice of militant nonviolence he embraced. And now, like Gandhi, Cesar announced that he would undertake a fast as an act of penitence and as a way of taking responsibility as a leader for his people.

The fast divided the UFW staff. Many didn't understand why Cesar was doing it. Others worried about his health. But the farmworkers understood. A mass was said nightly near where Cesar was fasting at the Forty Acres, the UFW's headquarters in Delano. Hundreds, then thousands, came. People pitched tents nearby. They brought religious offerings: pictures and small statues. Farmworkers waited in line for hours to speak with Cesar in his tiny room, while he refused interviews with reporters.

After twenty-five days, Cesar was carried to a nearby park where the fast ended during a mass with thousands of farmworkers. He had lost thirty-five pounds, but there was no more talk of violence among the farmworkers. Cesar's message had gotten through. Senator Robert Kennedy came to the mass, he said, "out of respect for one of the heroic figures of our time."

Cesar was too weak to speak, so his statement was read by others in both English and Spanish. "It is my deepest belief that only by giving our lives do we find life," they read. "The truest act of courage, the strongest act of manliness, is to sacrifice ourselves for others in a totally nonviolent struggle for justice. To be a man is to suffer for others. God help us to be men."

Cesar's efforts connected middleclass families in Northeastern cities and Midwestern suburbs with poor families in the hot California vineyards. Motivated by compassion, millions of people across North America stopped eating the grapes they had loved so much. At dinner tables across the country, parents gave their children a simple, powerful lesson in social justice by reaching out to those less fortunate than themselves. By 1970, the grape boycott was an unqualified success. Bowing to pressure from the boycott, grape growers at long last signed union contracts, granting workers human dignity and a more livable wage.

In the years that followed, Cesar continued to use strikes, boycotts, marches and fasts to help farmworkers stand up for their rights and to gather support from ordinary Americans to aid them in their efforts. In 1988, at the age of sixty-one, Cesar undertook his last public fast, this time for thirty-six days, to draw attention to the pesticide poisoning of farmworkers and their children.

By the values many use to measure success in the 1990s, Cesar Chavez was not very successful. He had been forced to quit school after the eighth grade to help his family. He never owned a house. He never earned more than $6,000 a year. When he died in 1993, at age sixty-six, he left no money for his family. Yet more than forty thousand people marched behind the plain pine casket at his funeral, honoring the more than forty years he spent struggling to improve the lives of farmworkers.

An all-night vigil was held under a giant tent before Cesar's funeral at Forty Acres, where his body lay in an open casket. Thousands and thousands of people filed by until morning. Parents carried newborn babies and sleeping toddlers in their arms. One farmworker explained, "I wanted to tell my children how they had once been in the presence of this great man."

What was the secret behind such a remarkable display? A reporter once asked Cesar, "What accounts for all the affection and respect so many farmworkers show you in public?" Cesar just looked down and smiled his easy smile. "The feeling is mutual" was his simple reply.

Marc Grossman has been with the UFW since the 1960s. He serves as the union's spokesperson.

It was a hot summer night in 1965 in the little San Joaquin Valley town of Delano, California. Cesar Chavez, with his shining black hair trailing across his forehead, wearing a green plaid shirt that had become almost a uniform, sat behind a makeshift desk topped with bright red Formica.

"*Sí se puede*," he said repeatedly to me, a highly skeptical reporter from San Francisco, as we talked deep into the early morning hours there in the cluttered shack that served as headquarters for him and the others who were trying to create an effective farmworkers union.

"*Sí se puede*—it can be done!"

But I would not be swayed. Too many others, over too many years, had tried and failed to win for farmworkers the union rights they had to have if they were to escape the severe economic and social deprivation inflicted on them by their grower employers.

The Industrial Workers of the World who stormed across Western fields early in the century, the Communists who followed, the socialists, the AFL and CIO organizers—all their efforts had collapsed under relentless pressure of growers and their powerful political allies.

I was certain this effort would be no different. I was wrong. I had not accounted for the brilliance, creativity, courage and stubbornness of Cesar Chavez, a sad-eyed, disarmingly soft-spoken man who talked of militancy in calm, measured tones, a gentle and incredibly patient man who hid great strategic talent behind shy smiles and an attitude of utter candor.

Chavez grasped the essential fact that farmworkers had to organize themselves. Outside organizers, however well-intentioned, could not do it. Chavez, a farmworker himself, carefully put together a grassroots organization that enabled the workers to form their own union, which then sought out—and won—widespread support from influential outsiders.

A small band heads up the dusty trail to Sacramento.

The key weapon of this United Farm Workers was the boycott. The UFW's grape boycott and others against wineries and lettuce growers won the first farm union contracts in history. And these boycotts led ultimately to enactment of the California law that required growers to bargain collectively with workers who voted for unionization and to substantial improvements in the pay, benefits and working conditions of the state's farmworkers.

The struggle was extremely difficult for the impoverished farmworkers, and Chavez risked his health—if not his life—to provide them extreme examples of the sacrifices necessary for victory. Most notably, he engaged in lengthy, highly publicized fasts that helped rally the public to the farmworkers' cause and that may very well have contributed to this untimely death in 1993.

Fasts, boycotts. It's no coincidence that these were among the principal tools of Mohandas Gandhi, for Chavez drew much of his inspiration from the Indian leader. Like Gandhi and another of his models, Martin Luther King, Jr., Chavez believed fervently in the tactics of nonviolence. Like them, he showed the world how profoundly effective these tactics can be in obtaining justice from even the most powerful of opponents.

What the UFW accomplished, and how the union accomplished it, will never be forgotten—not by the millions of social activists who have been inspired and energized by the farmworkers' struggle, nor by the workers themselves.

The UFW won vital legal rights and protections for them. But above all, farmworkers now have what Cesar Chavez insisted was needed above all else. That, he said, "is to have the worker truly believe, understand and know that he's free, that he's a free man, that he can stand up and say how he feels."

Freedom. No leader has ever left a greater legacy.

Dick Meister is coauthor of A *Long Time Coming: The Struggle to Unionize America's Farm Workers*.

It was early Friday afternoon and we were returning from a meeting with campesinos at Las Mercedes Coffee Cooperative in El Salvador over miles of rugged dirt road in beautiful mountain country when the car radio squawked that there was *"un mensaje urgente para la doctora"* (an urgent message for the doctor). When we arrived at the office an hour, later the secretary handed me a note written in pencil, *"Helen Chavez avisó que falleció Cesar Chavez"* (Helen Chavez wanted you to know that Cesar Chavez died). There was also an urgent message from the coroner in Bakersfield, California who was planning to do the autopsy that evening and wanted information from me, as Cesar's personal physician, about his past medical history.

When I got to the United Farm Workers headquarters in Keene and spoke with Helen, she told me that Cesar had died in his sleep in San Luis, Arizona. He was there to testify in a court retrial of the Bruce Church Industry case in Yuma and was staying at the home of a longtime union supporter. He had completed his testimony, having been on the stand for two full days. He went to bed around 10:00 P.M. on Thursday evening, April 22. At 8:00 A.M. on Friday morning, he had not come in for breakfast. David Martinez, the union officer who was travelling with Cesar and who was also staying at the house, knew how intense the testimony had been and how tired Cesar was from his hectic schedule and decided to let him sleep another hour. At 9:00 A.M. when David went in to wake Cesar, he found that though he seemed to be asleep, he was dead. Cesar died about twenty miles from Yuma, where he had been born sixty-six years earlier on March 31, 1927.

My first hours of grief were spent making arrangements to return to California from San Salvador, my mind teeming with memories of my long association with Cesar, whom I first met in October, 1965, at a meeting at the Unitarian Church in Berkeley when he came to ask for support for the grape workers who had gone out on strike in Delano on September 8. I remember some of what he said, but I mostly remember his gentle manner, and that, although he wasn't a

My flag, too.

Crossing the line to join La Huelga.

particularly good speaker, he had a strong moral force, an inner quality which the often-used word "charisma" cannot even begin to describe. Cesar Chavez would continue to be an inseparable part of my life and work through the coming years.

I left San Salvador early Saturday morning and read Cesar's obituary in six different newspapers before the day was over—in San Salvador, in two newspapers in Mexico City, in the *Los Angeles Times* and in the two San Francisco papers when I finally arrived home. All of the papers said that Cesar had died of natural causes. The Salvadoreno sitting next to me on the plane said that he didn't believe it was natural causes as the paper said, an attitude that I would find quite prevalent in the days ahead (the autopsy confirmed that he died of natural causes). I called Helen from Los Angeles and told her I would leave the next day for La Paz.

I drove through Pacheco Pass and down Highway 99 still not believing what I knew to be true, not wanting to see what I knew I would see when I arrived at La Paz—Cesar's lifeless body. So I kept trying to think of Cesar when he was alive, of his incredible energy, drive and commitment (which at close sight could not always be distinguished from obstinacy). I remembered the Friday night meetings at the Filipino Hall in Delano, especially the one where I noticed how much pain Cesar seemed to be in. I took care of him during his illness in 1969 when I called Dr. Janet Travell (President John Kennedy's doctor) whose treatment made him pain free after years of severe back pain. I remembered taking care of him during his first public fast in February, 1968, and many shorter ones, and his last public fast in August, 1988 which lasted thirty-six days. I remember how difficult and stubborn he could be (he said the same thing about me). We both usually ended up giving a little ground.

I remember one of the first questions Cesar ever asked me when he found out I was a nurse was "Do you know anything about pesticides?" Answering the question led to my leaving the union in 1971 to become a doctor. Pesticides were a major part of my work when I returned to work for the UFW from 1983 to 1986. I returned to my own practice in San Francisco but continued to work closely with Cesar and the union. My last public appearance with Cesar was in New York in December, 1992, for a national television show about pesticides and cancer in farmworker children.

Cesar was one of the most realistic persons I ever met. He understood exactly what the UFW was up against, and what it would take to change it. He was a man of clear vision and strong opinions whose superb organizing abilities, great personal integrity and commitment to nonviolence not only changed the way farmworkers thought about themselves, but also the way we thought about farmworkers. He did not believe in government handouts or legislation which invariably sanctified the status quo—a position amply justified by the failures of the California Agricultural Labor Relations Act passed in 1975. He didn't believe in top-down problem solving, and never lost touch with the workers.

Working with the UFW meant extraordinary personal demands and sacrifices and the need to sustain a high level of commitment over the long-term. The inspiring and the lofty were mixed with a much greater amount of the tedious and mundane. It was not always easy to adjust or sort it all out,

Strawberry fields forever…and forever…and forever.

and over the years, many left the union in varying stages of confusion, bewilderment or turmoil.

Cesar was a living example that if you never forget the people, if you don't get distracted, and if you can keep your sense of social justice intact, you won't be lost along the way. You won't burn out and you can make impossible things happen. He broke the cycle of hopelessness, pessimism and despair. There are millions whose lives were touched by Cesar because he showed us a way to do good, to join the struggle, even if only by the simple yet profound act of not buying grapes.

Marion Moses, M.D. is president of the Pesticide Education Center, San Francisco, California.

We deliver your peas cheap.

My family and I were working to organize the United Farm Workers' third grape boycott in New York City when I received a call from Helen Chavez, Cesar's wife, on a Monday morning in July, 1988. She calmly explained that Cesar had driven himself to the UFW's Forty Acres, which hosts the union's operations in Delano, California, moved into a small room and begun a water-only fast. Helen had no idea how long he planned to go without food, but she was concerned because Cesar was now sixty-one years old.

His first long public fast had occurred more than twenty years before when he was forty-one. When it ended after twenty-five days in 1968, the late Senator Robert F. Kennedy flew to Delano to be by Cesar's side, calling the UFW founder "one of the heroic figures of our time."

After the first few days of the 1988 fast, I left to be with Cesar and my family followed shortly thereafter. When I arrived in California on the sixth day, I wasn't quite sure what to expect. However, Cesar was very clear about the purpose of his fast.

He called it a "Fast for Love." He saw the fast as a way to educate the American people about the tragedies that cancer- and birth defect-causing pesticides visit on the children living in agricultural communities. I was worried how this message would get out beyond Delano, which was a small, largely farmworker community of 40,000 people in northern Kern County, hundreds of miles from any major media market.

But during those weeks in the summer of 1988, Cesar taught me, as he did on so many occasions, the power and strength of nonviolent sacrifice. Cesar was very disciplined. He would take only water during the fast. He refused to speak with reporters. His only contact with the public was his attendance at a daily 7:00 P.M. Catholic mass, in which he participated up until the last week of the fast when he became too weak. Towards the end, it was all Cesar could do to conserve his energy so he was able to attend mass.

My initial concerns about getting Cesar's message out to the public from this out-of-the-way place were put to rest as people from all walks of life began traveling to Delano to demonstrate their support for the children of farmworkers who were suffering from pesticides. Ethel Kennedy, widow of Robert Kennedy, many of the Kennedy children, as well as entertainment industry figures, labor and religious leaders, including the Reverend Jesse Jackson, politicians and tens of thousands of farmworkers joined Cesar during those thirty-six days.

The state and national press also came in growing numbers to follow events and report on Cesar's declining condition.

It was extremely difficult to watch his strength diminish by the day. But Cesar's spirit never wavered. As the fast stretched, his physical condition deteriorated so that you had to lean over so he could whisper in your ear. The doctors who were attending him were very concerned that he could be doing permanent damage to his health.

By then, all of us were deeply worried. Over a four-week period, we witnessed this giant of a man physically reduced almost to the point where he was courting death.

On August 21, 1988, Cesar broke his fast during a mass held in a mammoth tent at Forty Acres and attended by thousands of farmworkers and their supporters. He was so weak that two of Cesar's sons, Paul and Anthony, had to virtually carry him to and from his seat.

Even years later, the Fast for Love is cherished in the hearts of so many people who witnessed those moving moments. It reflected the commitment and determination of one man to bring a critical issue before the public conscience.

It was such actions that made Cesar unique. At a time when so few people seemed willing to risk their careers, much less their lives, on behalf of principle, Cesar was ready to sacrifice himself totally to improve the lives of people suffering in our society—especially the children. By his own example, he was always challenging you to do a little bit more than you were already doing. He truly gave every ounce of energy to *La Causa*, the cause.

In his first major speech after recovering from the fast, in March, 1989, at Pacific Lutheran University in Tacoma, Washington, Cesar said the fast "was for those who know they could or should do more...The times we face truly call for all of us to do more to stop this evil in our midst. The answer lies with you and me. It is with all men and women who share the suffering and yearn with us for a better world.

"Our cause goes on in hundreds of distant places," he concluded. "It multiplies among thousands and then millions of caring people who heed through a multitude of simple deeds the commandment set out in the book of the Prophet Micah, in the Old Testament: 'What does the Lord require of you, but to do justice, to love kindness, and to walk humbly with your God.'"

That passage from Micah could well serve as Cesar's own epitaph.

Veteran United Farm Workers organizer Arturo S. Rodriguez succeeded Cesar Chavez as president of the UFW in May, 1993.

I used to tell people that I'd never loved nor hated anyone as much as I did Cesar Chavez. During the thirty-one years Cesar was in my life, I sometimes thought he was the most Christ-like man I'd ever met. But when we crossed verbal swords, I'd become infuriated or wounded. I expected so much—too much—from him because his capacity for giving was extraordinary. I expected he could fix my life as well as the lives of thousands of farmworkers. And, of course, although he did help me evolve, that wasn't his top priority.

After I left the farmworkers' movement, we sustained our friendship. In fact, he seemed more like my other friends at that point, not the world-renowned person he actually was. When Cesar and his companion Mike Ybarra arrived to spend a night at our home at the end of a long day, they seemed to appreciate forgetting about the union for a couple of hours, watching "The Johnny Carson Show" or talking about our children or politics. Sometimes he surprised me by washing dishes without being asked.

When you peel away the numbers of innovative contracts he signed, awards he received and rumors about the man—all those trappings of the myth of Cesar Estrada Chavez—you unwrap perhaps his finest legacy. That is, he admonished us to understand that to be perfectly human is to be imperfect. That we cannot avoid wrestling with demons as an ongoing challenge. And that we must celebrate every victory as we drag people into a progressively more humane sphere—whether at the individual level or, as was Cesar's privilege, by the thousands.

From the spring of 1971 through the fall of 1973, Susan Samuels Drake served as Cesar's secretary.

Going down this long, hard road.

Home, sweet home.

I first met Cesar Chavez in the early 1960s. He came to our house in Parlier, California to talk to us about a union for farmworkers.

I was very impressed with him.

He was the first person to tell us that women were equal to men and that we had the same rights. That we should stand side-by-side and demand our rights.

Cesar was a very quiet man. At meetings he didn't tell us what to do. He would talk to us and explain many of the things that were happening and that it was up to us to decide for ourselves. He never raised his voice to us except when he remembered the injustices against farmworkers.

Cesar was very kind, understood our problems and tried to advise us.

I remember being a person who did my work, even though I knew that I was being taken advantage of by the labor contractors who kept part of our wages. I did not dare complain for fear of being fired. But from Cesar I learned how to defend myself and others.

He encouraged me to testify at hearings on minimum wages for women, sanitation out in the fields, banning the short-handled hoe and of the necessity of food stamps for the needy in Fresno.

I traveled far and near to testify on behalf of farmworkers. Because of that I was invited to speak at universities, churches and other unions, seeking support for our cause.

Cesar always told us that we were a very large family and should look after each other.

He changed my life and any good that I do for others will be in his memory.

His passing away affected many people, but it was a greater loss to us, the farmworkers who knew him and will never forget him; he will be in our hearts forever.

I say he changed me because before knowing and hearing him, I did not know who I was—only a housewife, mother and farmworker. Now I can identify myself as a woman proud of my heritage and know what I can do to help myself and others. Now I can talk politics and everyday things that affect us.

I'm so glad to have known him and his wonderful family.

Jessie De La Cruz is recognized as one of the first female organizers to form a farmworker committee.

My hands are calloused from the hoe.

As time goes on, many people will say many things about Cesar, but I think the story that best states the feelings of many, including my own, is this one:

It was the day of the actual funeral and tens of thousands of people had come from around the world to pay their last respects to a truly special spirit. I stood holding a camera ready to document the day's events along with seven other filmmakers who had all volunteered their services. I was speaking to Cesar's eldest son and he was recounting a situation which had just occurred.

It seems that Mrs. Robert Kennedy had arrived at the local airport and was being escorted from the plane. Upon her stepping onto the tarmac, she was quickly asked if she wanted to speak to some of the press who had assembled or did she want to wait to get to the main press area at the memorial site. She chose to start answering questions immediately.

The first question asked was, "Cesar has been compared to your late husband Robert Kennedy and to Martin Luther King, Jr. What do you think of that?"

Without missing a beat, she immediately stated, "Oh no, you can't do that, for you see, Cesar was a saint."

The beginning.

Edward James Olmos is an activist, actor and author.

We, father and son, see a future.

The only famous person who ever befriended me was Cesar Chavez. Unlike what we hear about celebrities, however, he was as unassuming, humble and smart as he has been made out to be. In 1974, he stayed in my house in Gainesville, Florida. This was an ordinary suburban house of a middle-level faculty member, a working wife and two small children. He ate at our table with no menu demands whatever. The only special treatment was to provide vegetables for a juicer machine that was brought along. He was even reluctant to take our bedroom. There was no celebrity treatment or fanfare.

In 1988, in the midst of huge pressures on United Farm Workers, I was to be in Irvine, California on business and called to ask if I could come up to La Paz to see Cesar. He was in meetings but sent the message that of course I would be welcome. He was still recovering from his long fast that year, so we met while he was working his little garden. He greeted me as a friend and we talked at length. Of course we discussed his condition, his emotional state, his sense of the prospects for UFW. But he also wanted to know about me and about my sons. I was the one honored, yet he expressed gratitude that I would come.

Years earlier, also at La Paz, when my older son was almost four, the first lettuce boycott was in full operation. Nonetheless, Cesar took the time to walk with the little boy's hand in his and listened carefully as my son asked him about a bumper sticker on our car. Pointing to the sticker, Matthew asked in toddler Spanish, "¿Sabes Cesar que dice?" ("Do you know what that says, Cesar?"). Cesar said, "¿Que dice Mateito?" ("What does it say, little Matthew?"). Matthew said, "Dice no compre chuga."—correctly "No compre lechuga," that is, "Don't buy lettuce." Cesar's response was to congratulate Matthew for his commitment to helping farmworkers and continued the conversation for several more minutes.

Cesar was not an electrifying public speaker—yet he commanded attention and respect and people remembered his message. His persuasiveness and authenticity with workers were stunning to witness. Like lots of bright people, his mistakes usually were big ones. I sometimes did not agree with him about UFW's Florida strategy and later about the focus of UFW's direct mail efforts in the 1980s. He knew that but did not shut me out.

Even his errors seem to have come from the intensity of his unswerving commitment to justice for farmworkers (and not fame for himself). More than a few people got burned out by that intensity, combined with the constant crisis in which UFW had to live for almost thirty years, but no one could argue that Cesar did not demand as much of himself. His sense of vocation and calling was a manifestation of the deep faith that marked him and had a powerful influence on others, including me.

Cesar had a sense of humor that he used both to reassure people and teach them. The National Farm Worker Ministry asked many of us to come help with the Cochella strike in 1973. Among other duties, I was translating on picket lines for national United Auto Workers' staff. The picketing was restricted by many complicated injunctions and orders. Law enforcement was hostile and the Teamster counter-pickets were pretty frightening. At one point a deputy brushed by and jostled one of the farmworkers in our line. It happened that Cesar arrived shortly afterwards. When he was told of the little incident, he asked the worker, with that little grin, if he'd fallen. The worker said no, it wasn't anything. Cesar said "Next time, fall down."

"Huh? Why?" asked the bewildered worker.

"You're trying to draw the foul, man!" said Cesar without missing a beat and then he started chuckling. A quick lesson in militant, nonviolent protest had just been taught.

And last, I will remember always that he respected his friends. Some in La Causa pressed me pretty hard to leave "that science stuff" and "the irrelevant university life" and come do "something real." Cesar never did. He always said that he was glad to have friends and supporters in many walks of life. He congratulated me when I was tenured and promoted and again when a "teacher of the year" award came to me. Of all the famous people that might have befriended me, it is a wonderful memory—but a sense of sharp loss still—that my famous friend was Cesar Chavez.

Samuel B. Trickey has been a supporter of farmworker organizing and the United Farm Workers since the 1966 watermelon strike in his home state of Texas.

Authority has its limits.

Cesar, for me, was a grand teacher and friend. I admired him very much. He had such a fine manner in getting things done. It wasn't necessary for him to speak. His actions taught us a lot. By being himself, he convinced the world of the need to help in the cause.

Cesar was protected by God. That's why everyone wanted to help him.

For one and a half years, I was one of Cesar's bodyguards. I was with him day and night. One night, he was awake at two in the morning. I asked, "Can't you sleep?" His response was, "I'm praying for the children. I can never get to it during the day."

Alfredo Vazquez, worked for the UFW from 1968–1980.

Self-empowerment for self-improvement.

For most of the time that I worked with the farmworkers' movement, I was employed by an ecumenical church organization. From 1961–71, I was director of the California Migrant Ministry and from 1971–81, executive director of the National Farm Worker Ministry. Beginning with the Delano strike in 1965, our ministry focused more and more on the needs, goals and campaigns of the National Farm Workers Association/United Farm Workers of America.

Cesar began organizing the staff and leadership of the California Migrant Ministry in the 1950s and he intensified that effort when he started to build the National Farm Workers' Association in 1962. In my naiveté in the early 60s, I sometimes wondered why he took the time to meet with me in Delano and to attend our CMM staff retreats. It was a lonely task he had begun, so I speculated that fellowship may have been his motivation. But looking back, I am sure he knew he would need allies when the first strikes came, and he was carefully preparing us to be among those allies.

During all the years that I was the leader of a parallel church-sponsored organization, Cesar carefully and consistently respected the fact that the CMM/NFWM was a separate entity with a board of directors of our own, a constituency of our own and financial struggles of our own. When he needed a major piece of help from us, he always called me personally to explain the situation and/or crisis and to ask for exactly what was needed. He expected me to say yes, which I probably always did. Occasionally we negotiated a response that would be more realistic for the churches, but that seldom happened because Cesar had a very clear and down-to-earth view of what we could do.

I have often wondered how many "no's" or "maybes" from me would have ended those phone calls. Probably very few!

One other event reminds me of Cesar, the practical organizer. It was the summer of 1973. The grape growers had announced that they were unilaterally dropping their UFW contracts and signing with the Teamsters. The workers went on strike, first in the Coachella Valley. The Teamsters sent some of their largest, toughest members from all over the state to protect the fields and the scabs working the fields—and to intimidate the strikers and the UFW organizers. It was a tense, frightening time for everyone. We in the NFWM had invited a number of church members and leaders to be present to help keep the peace—but peace was a fleeting thing in the summer of 1973.

One day in June, 1973, I received a call from the Reverend John Moyer, a longtime friend of the farmworkers' movement and an NFWM board member. John told me that the General Synod of the United Church of Christ was meeting in St. Louis. There were over a thousand delegates and visitors in attendance. John wanted to know if they should send a delegation from St. Louis to Coachella. I, of course, said, "Yes!" I also told him, "The sooner the better!" John and his colleagues organized a group of ninety-five delegates representing every conference (state level organizations) in the nation—some familiar with the farmworkers' struggle and some with little or no knowledge. They also chartered a plane to fly this delegation to Coachella. It was a better plan than we could have expected. But before the group took off, John called me back. He told me that some of the leaders of the church had been rethinking this plan. Considering buses in St. Louis, the charter plane, food and buses in California, this project was going to cost nearly $25,000. Wouldn't the UFW prefer to have the money instead of the delegation? I told John that I was pretty sure Cesar would say, "Send the delegation!" but I also promised to double-check. Cesar took about fifteen seconds to think about his answer. He told me, "Please ask them to send the people. After twenty-four hours here in Coachella we will have ninety-five new church organizers spread throughout the country." And so the plane-load of UCC delegates came to Coachella. The strikers welcomed them with open hearts and open arms. The Teamsters did their macho best to intimidate the visitors. And Cesar's prediction about new organizers came true.

The Reverend Wayne "Chris" Hartmire is head of Loaves & Fishes in Sacramento, California.

We're just passing through.

My wife Liz and I had been interested in the union for years and had discussed the possibility of joining the movement full-time. In December, 1972, we flew to California to spend a week with the workers. At that time we talked with dozens of people who were working at the headquarters—some Chicanos who had grown up in the fields, some middle class Anglos like ourselves.

We were interviewed by Dolores Huerta, one of Chavez' closest associates and later spent two relaxed hours with Cesar in his home. To both of them we expressed our misgivings. The characteristic we most noticed among the staffers was their great intensity. Liz and I aren't very intense folks, and we wanted to have time to relax now and then.

Cesar thought we could work that out for ourselves and, after some discussion, he invited us to come and work. We returned to our home in Washington, D.C. to think it over. After a few weeks we decided to go.

We gave notice to our employers, rented out our newly purchased house and sold all our furniture. We piled what we needed into and on top of our small car and, like the migrants we were about to join, traveled across the country.

We got mixed reactions from relatives and friends along the way. Some thought we were foolhardy to relinquish security at our ages (I was forty-four, Liz was forty). Others thought we were heroes. I suppose we were a little of both.

We laugh now at the reception we got when we arrived in California. The union's offices were located near the tiny town of Keene in what used to be a tuberculosis hospital. There were more than a hundred acres and several rambling and ramshackle buildings. The entrance gate was always guarded. We drove up to the gate, halfway expecting the Tijuana Brass Band to welcome us after our journey. Instead the guard told us to wait until someone could come down and identify us. We cooled our heels in the car for forty-five minutes until someone broke away from work and came to admit us.

Our arrival had been expected, and we hoped we could settle in quickly. We were taken to the old hospital building and shown a room which was unoccupied. It was covered with trash and had a broken bed, a broken window and a stopped-up sink. We refused it (we were beginning to get peeved) and went in search of another room. We found one at the end of a corridor. It was piled with broken furniture and empty beer cans, had ancient obscenities scribbled on the walls, but it did have windows and a sink that worked.

We set to work to clean it up and after several hours had gotten rid of the trash, mopped the floors, brought in a couple of beds from other rooms and ensconced ourselves. When the girl in charge of new arrivals came to tell us we couldn't have that room, we told her we'd move when we got time. We were learning fast.

The bathroom and shower were down the corridor. We soon found that toilet paper left in the bathroom disappeared and we learned to carry our own. Occasionally, only occasionally, did the shower produce hot water.

After four months in this room, Liz and I moved up in seniority and were able to move into half of a small bungalow. We had only two tiny rooms and a bath but at last our toilet paper was safe.

Living conditions like that resulted from Chavez' determination to keep the union a genuine organ of the poor. For him, it was unthinkable that representatives of the poor be better off than those for whom they labor. Housing was provided, but most staff people, Cesar included, got $7.50 a week for food and $5.00 for other expenses. As a result, the union was staffed only by those with a strong and sincere interest in social justice.

The Chavez family lived in an extremely simple, small, frame house. The only indication that it was theirs was the high chain link fence which surrounded the yard. Cesar was a poor man fighting for poor men.

The tension of the work often left little time for interpersonal niceties, and property was sometimes considered available for the community when left lying around.

We are etched by the earth.

Then there was the work itself. Liz was assigned to the administration of the union's medical program and I to the producing and marketing of farmworker literature. Our jobs were enjoyable and challenging and we were given all the freedom and responsibility we could expect. But despite our efforts to preserve some time for ourselves, our jobs soon came to be our entire existence. The scheduled workweek was fifty-three hours but it was always necessary to work overtime. We were almost constantly exhausted.

Besides the scheduled job, there was picket duty for staffers. Cesar was concerned that the administrative people not withdraw into an ivory tower and that they value their paperwork only in terms of the people they served. Every person was pressured to take his place on the picket line when the union was on strike. This entailed rising at 4:00 A.M., driving some forty miles and walking a picket line outside an orchard or vineyard. We would be strung out on a country road for a quarter of a mile, twenty, thirty or fifty feet apart, according to the injunction of the local court. We would have to stay on the side of the road opposite the field where the strikebreakers were working.

Across the road, between us and the workers, would be a line of Teamster strong-arm men imported from Los Angeles and paid $67.50 a day. There were always armed, private policemen with the Teamsters, hired by the growers to "protect" their workers.

We would shout to the workers, asking them not to break our strike and to come out and join us. The Teamsters would shout too so the workers could not hear what we said. Sometimes they would set up a loudspeaker system and play blaring music to drown us out. Often things would deteriorate to the point where we and the Teamsters would simply trade insults across the road.

We had the sympathy of many of the scab workers. Even though for economic reasons they could or would not join the strike, they often picked green fruit or deliberately bruised it so the growers' profits were cut.

Violence erupted now and then, but never, repeat never, as United Farm Workers' policy. Chavez' determination to bring about social change through nonviolence is one of the things that made him the great leader he was.

Chavez wanted not just a decent wage. He wanted farmworkers, educated and uneducated, white, black and brown, to be accepted as human beings by their employers and to have the power to control their own lives.

Certain evenings, and on Sundays, administrative staffers were encouraged to go to a neighboring town to distribute leaflets in front of grocery stores that were marketing nonunion produce. Trying to turn shoppers away from stores was often a bruising experience. People were insulting and called us anything from communists to parasites and suggested we leave the country or get a job. Leaflet distribution would continue until the store closed at 10:00 P.M.

Liz and I did not go very often to picket the ranches or to pass out leaflets at the stores. We were just too tired. But many of the staff went almost every day besides doing their regular administrative work.

Cesar was a wonder. He was often at his office at 3:00 A.M. to read correspondence and dictate replies before the staff arrived. He worked intently all day, rarely napping in the afternoon. He traveled an enormous amount, visiting various union offices or flying across the country to speaking engagements and rallies. He was a vegetarian and obtained his immense physical energy largely from fruit and raw vegetables.

When he talked of his plans for the future, his eyes would light up with anticipation. His confidence was contagious. He knew he would succeed. He often said time will accomplish for the poor what money does for the rich.

There was an unmistakable religious aspect to the union. It was a modern crusade led by a man with what seemed to be almost a divine mandate to lead the poor out of bondage. A great number of full-time volunteers were former ministers, priests or sisters, and some religious communities had given permission for members to work for the UFW. I think many religious people found in the union a vigor and purity they missed in the traditional ministries of the church.

Community meetings often began with a prayer. On one occasion Jim Drake, a minister who had worked with the union since its inception in 1964, was asked to lead the prayer. Everyone bowed his head expectantly. Jim's powerful voice split the silence, "Lord, don't let the bastards wear us down." There were as many vivas as amens.

After leaving La Paz in 1974, Bob and Liz Maxwell returned to Washington, D.C. to work as clinical social workers and in various social justice movements.

Many candles of hope overcome the darkness.

During the late 1960s, I lived in Saginaw, Michigan. We had visited migrant camps and we were in awe of the leadership of Cesar Chavez. On one picket line, someone handed my three-year-old son Paul a sign which read, "Grapes are Evil."

Soon after moving to Washington, D.C., I joined the local boycott staff of the UFW as a fund-raiser in the churches in the D.C. area. While visiting Washington, Cesar and his bodyguard stayed with our family. My six children ranged in age from three to nine. Sons Jim and Paul, six and seven years old, worshipped Cesar. They did not want me to change the sheets of the bed in which Cesar had slept.

During the boycott era, I remember a mass honoring Cesar at the home of Eunice and Sargent Shriver. Hundreds of people attended, and there was a lot of food. The meat was cooked in holes in the ground for a couple of days, farmworker style. All of the children played together in the pool—farmworker children, volunteers' children and the Kennedy and Shriver children. This was one of the fruits of the efforts of Cesar Chavez.

Another occasion I recall was the movie premiere of the life of Woody Guthrie, *Bound for Glory*. We packed the Jenifer Theatre in Washington, D.C. Cesar was there as well as Arlo Guthrie, Arlo's mother Marjorie and David Carradine who played the role of Guthrie. The unions all participated by buying blocks of tickets. The evening turned out to be a once-in-a-lifetime event.

From 1972 to 1992, I was with Cesar at times when he was fasting and times when he was eating his regular vegetarian diet. Once in a while we would go out for Chinese food and share some California wine of his choosing. When Cesar fasted, he thought and spoke with great clarity, as I remember him doing when I picked him up at National Airport one snowy night in the late 70s. At the time, I was membership coordinator for the National Association of Farmworker Organizations, and the Carter administration was granting federal funds to farmworker organizations for their projects. The UFW decided to join NAFO. One of the lasting outcomes of its membership was a grant for a farmworker radio station.

In the early 1980s, I was asked to be the UFW's lobbyist in Washington, D.C. I had an office in the AFL-CIO building on 16th Street and met with all of the union's legislative personnel each Monday morning. I worked very closely with Dolores Huerta and Cesar's son Paul. The most challenging legislation was the Simpson-Mazzoli Immigration bill. There was a lot of controversy between the Hispanic community and the unions over sanctioning employers who hired illegal aliens. Cesar really listened to me in discussing all sides of this issue and trusted me to testify and to do the right thing.

One afternoon, we picked Cesar up at the George Meany Center for Labor Studies. When we arrived, he was finishing his packing. Lo and behold, this great leader was rolling each item of clothing and placing them in the suitcase in perfect order. "Helen taught me to do this," he said, lest I give him total credit.

Cesar was a Raiders fan when they were the Oakland Raiders. One evening, my son Paul was watching the Raiders game with Cesar on "Monday Night Football." Paul asked Cesar why he would be a fan of such a violent team, to which Cesar responded, "That's simple, Paul, the Raiders are supporters of the union."

My eldest grandson Bobby was crying uncontrollably one morning while Cesar was holding a meeting in our dining room. Cesar asked what was wrong. I told him that I was quite sure that the baby was overtired. Cesar picked him up, held him close, walked up and down the hallway and within minutes Bobby was sleeping.

Stephanie Blondis Bower was both a friend of Cesar and a longtime UFW supporter.

I find myself in La Causa.

Americans, we.

I started working with the union in 1974 when I was seventeen years old. After working on the Los Angeles boycott for about a year and a half, my boyfriend, Elizer Vasquez, was reassigned to La Paz to participate in an auto mechanic training program. Anyway, I got to follow along, and since I wasn't very well known at La Paz, Cesar had me work with Esther Padilla in the service center for a few days. (I didn't realize it at the time, but this was his way of finding out what kind of worker I was and of getting an idea of my skills before giving me a permanent assignment.)

Esther asked me to try to make sense of all the service center property tax bills, which, typically, were in a real mess. I spent three days figuring out which bills had been paid already and ended up with a schedule for all twenty-six properties, showing amounts due and tax deadlines.

After Cesar returned from his road trip, he called me into his office for a meeting. I remember being so thrilled at finally meeting him that I was totally caught off guard when he asked me to work on his staff!

At the time, Cesar had one secretary and four administrative assistants whose job it was to act as liaisons between Cesar and the department heads. I was given the job of administrative assistant to the president and worked in that capacity for a year. We had daily morning meetings with Cesar and were present at all of his meetings with the department heads. It was a wonderful way to learn the internal workings of the union and also an incredible opportunity to watch Cesar in action.

There are a couple of incidents that I remember from that year of working on Cesar's staff. Neither one of them is especially earth-shattering, but I think they give a glimpse of what Cesar was really like.

The first took place when I got a call about 2:00 A.M. at home. Cesar wanted me to come to a meeting in his office to take some notes for him. Jerry Cohen had been renegotiating one of the contracts and he was calling to give Cesar a report on the negotiations and get input on whether to settle or not. I was half asleep but woke up pretty fast walking to the office in the cold Tehachapi air.

When I got there, Cesar was already at his desk, and the other executive board members who were at La Paz at the time started trudging in. Jerry called and Cesar put him on the speaker phone so that we could all hear. Dolores Huerta, Gilbert Padilla, Richard Chavez and Peter Velasco were the other board members present.

The phone call went on for about two hours with a lot of questions from everyone present and an air of genuine excitement because the negotiations, which had been difficult, were finally coming to a close. During that phone conversation I got a glimpse of what a tough negotiator Cesar was. He kept grilling Jerry, asking at various points whether Jerry felt satisfied that he had gotten the very best he could for the workers. Cesar also paid great attention to detail, going through the entire contract, from wages and working conditions to benefits. As the phone call came to an end, we all went home to bed for a couple hours of sleep. It went without saying that Cesar would be back in his office at 8:00 A.M. and he expected all of us to be at work as well.

One of the first things that really impressed me about Cesar was that he never seemed fatigued. He said that he rarely slept more than three hours a night. He used to joke that those of us who were less than half his age couldn't keep up with him. He brought a great deal of energy to the work and inspired us by example. He worked long, hard hours and always kept sight of the fact that no matter how tough the union work seemed at times, the workers in the field had it much worse. He took the responsibility of leading the union very seriously.

Cesar was tenacious and could be incredibly stubborn. At times, meetings seemed to go on forever. He really liked knowing what was going on. Sometimes his demands for detail and hands-on management drove those of us working under him nuts. But he was tremendously confident in his abilities. He liked to be involved on the ground level. He was wary of experts. He was self-taught and although he had little formal schooling, he was one of the most well-rounded and educated people I have ever met. He had a clear vision of what he wanted to win for the farmworkers, and he would never accept "It can't be done" for an answer. He'd react by saying, "There's a way. You just haven't figured it out yet. Come back when you have."

The second incident that stands out in the year I worked as administrative assistant to Cesar occurred one night when I had gone back to work after dinner. Cesar came into the office and was surprised to find me there still working. He really startled me when he said, "It's late. Why don't you go home?" Coming from a workaholic who pushed himself hard and who demanded as much from those who worked with him, this really shocked me. When I asked him why he had said that, he responded, "You can only get so much done in a day. Sometimes it's better to go home and get some rest so you can come back fresh the next day."

I think Cesar sensed I was tired. What he was telling me was that you need to pace yourself if you're going to be around for the long haul. It was good advice, and I'm sure something that he'd had to deal with personally over the years. It was also an example of how he interacted with people. As driven as he was to get the work done, he also cared on a personal level.

Later, when I was a department head, and was meeting with him less frequently, he never failed to ask how my kids were at the start of the meetings. He might be tough (and usually was) if you hadn't been able to make as much progress on a work assignment as he wanted, but he separated that quite easily from his personal relationship with you. I think that sense of genuine caring is what inspired us to keep working day in and day out.

Terry Vasquez Scott worked for the union from 1974 until 1988. Her job assignments were the Los Angeles boycott, Cesar's staff, NFWSC, the Seattle boycott, the St. Louis boycott, the Kansas City boycott, the Detroit boycott and the accounting department.

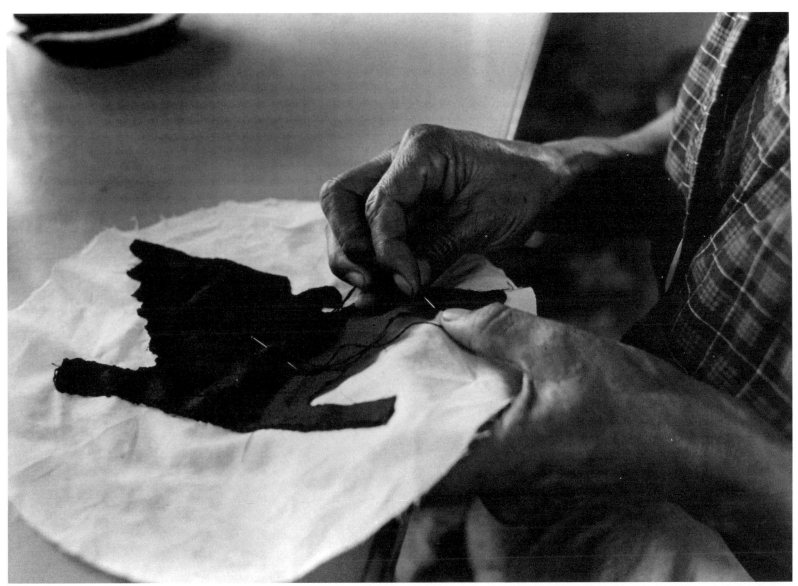

Stitches for justice.

Clear eyes,
deep understanding.

I worked at Forty Acres in Delano and at La Paz in the Tehachapi mountains. Community meetings were a part of our experience. They were more formal at Forty Acres where the participants came from various areas and the agenda was more business oriented. In La Paz we were a smaller and more closely knit group so a more informal, family-like atmosphere prevailed. I always looked forward to the meetings, especially when Cesar was going to be present. It was always exciting when Cesar was around. He updated us on the union, the progress of the national grape and lettuce boycotts and, closer to home in California, coming marriages, births, birthdays and introductions of new volunteers, etc.

Problems, too, were addressed. I remember that some baby clothes were reported missing from the common laundry, and Cesar was extremely serious about the matter. We were a family and this kind of action would not be tolerated. Though very kind, he knew how to be firm and everyone knew he meant what he said.

Once, a question about using the swimming pool came up, since workers in other areas didn't have access to such a luxury. In the end, I think only the children used it.

The meetings always concluded when Cesar rattled his keys. The guard dogs Huelga and Boycott leaped to their feet and were off with their master.

I believe Cesar made accountability a priority for himself and required it of others. While working on the books, I saw two items recorded that remain in my memory—the amount spent on dog food was well recorded, as was the price of his daughter's graduation dress. One summer I sorted out boxes and boxes of receipts—parking lot stubs, hair cuts, fast food, etc. We were preparing archival materials to be sent to Wayne State University, the official archives for the United Farm Workers.

Women, children and the elderly were issues of concern in our society and for Cesar back in the 1970s. I was delighted when I was allowed to come to work an hour earlier so I could

This is not the America I was taught.

help lay the tile on the roof of the new clinic—the clinic where I saw babies born and the medical needs of women and children met with the marvelous services of young volunteer doctors.

A retirement home was built with the elderly Filipino workers in mind. These men, many of whom were bachelors, had no families, and Cesar's concern was to care for them and offer them a sense of security in their golden years.

I believe the common good was always one of Cesar's objectives. He worked tirelessly, nonviolently and prayerfully that the dignity of all human beings, but especially the farmworkers, would be recognized and acted upon. Cesar's life reflects Micah 6:8, to act justly, to love tenderly and to walk humbly with your God.

Sister Beth Wood is based in Rome, Italy.

Should I join?
Do I have a choice?

Cesar got your attention. A slight, soft-spoken man with unremarkable features, he was a unique motivator. Cesar had a mystical power of suggestion. Wordlessly, he could make you decide—on the spot—that his focus and his interests ought to become your own. You wanted to work with him. This was the source of his genius.

I recall meeting Cesar for the first time in January, 1972. My wife Barbara and I were greeted by him in his office at La Paz. Dressed in simple, practical attire, he was cordial and brief in his welcome. I knew immediately it was time to get to work. We moved our two children and our belongings into two small rooms in an old TB sanitarium on the property that served as the UFW headquarters, and got to work.

There was plenty of work to do. Cesar expected every aspect of the union's life to be centrally controlled. All of the union's resources, all organizing campaigns, all initiatives of any kind were directed by department heads who were to have daily contact with Cesar and who were accountable to him. For years this arrangement worked effectively. Much got done this way. Centralized management worked well because of the competence and full-time dedication of the people placed in charge of large areas of the union's work. Department heads took their orders from Cesar and then would delegate large tasks into daily work routines for the La Paz staff and for all of the union's scattered personnel.

Soon after our arrival at La Paz, we attended the first of many community meetings. At these gatherings reports were given and news shared about the union's activities. Cesar or one of the other department heads presided at these meetings, which were sometimes conducted in Spanish and English. They included singing, progress reports and plans for community life at La Paz. The meetings were all well planned, complete with an agenda which was drawn with large markers on butcher paper and hung on the wall. These events helped keep the La Paz community organized and reminded us all that we were at the center of an extensive team of dedicated workers.

We soon moved our family from the hospital to a trailer and settled into a work week of five and a half days, plus the evening meetings. Attendance was expected.

In our time, a community garden was an important concern. Everyone worked in the garden on Saturday mornings.

I could have stayed on that scrubby, picturesque hillside forever. But, like countless others, one campaign or crisis after another caused us to be shifted around the country. After four months at La Paz, working first as a delinquent loan collections agent for the credit union and then as a bus driver, I was sent to Arizona to help confront a dangerous farm labor law. After Arizona, we were moved to Missouri for boycott organizing, to Florida to build church support, then back to St. Louis. There were also campaigns in Los Angeles and Salinas, including field elections, contract administration and staff training. During these years there were brief returns to La Paz.

Wherever the work carried us, Cesar's active presence was felt. Sometimes he showed up for the sake of local or regional publicity or to see for himself what was going on. One was always accountable, weekly or even daily, for specific tasks. You called in to La Paz or you were called. Sometimes Cesar himself called.

Cesar had a grand imagination and was the grand experimenter with whom you wanted to work.

The Reverend Richard Cook, a Baptist minister and attorney, was on the staff of the National Farm Workers Ministry from 1972 until 1983.

"When we are really honest with ourselves, we must admit that our lives are all that truly belong to us. So it is how we use our lives that determines what kind of men we are. It is my deepest belief that only by giving our lives do we find life. I am convinced that the truest act of courage, the strongest act of manliness, is to sacrifice ourselves for others in a totally nonviolent struggle for justice. To be a man is to suffer for others. God help us to be men."

— *Cesar Chavez*

I remember one bright day sometime after my retirement in 1988. I was cutting the grass between the roses with a Weed Eater. Cesar came to talk to me and told me of his appreciation of my caring for the rose garden and cutting the weeds around the community.

I said "Thank you," then continued cutting the grass. He did not leave but stood at a distance watching me cut the grass. After awhile I thought he would like to talk to me some more, so I stopped and asked him, "Do you want to see me?"

"No," he replied. "I am fascinated by how nicely you cut the grass." Then he left.

Little did we know then that I was trimming the grass at his future grave site. (Cesar was buried in the rose garden at La Paz.) It's funny how events work. Moments and events talk in a mysterious way. We don't understand now, but later.

I met Cesar for the first time at the Filipino Community Hall in Delano, California in September, 1965, after his members and board decided to join with the Filipino strikers of Agricultural Workers Organizing Committee AFL-CIO under the leadership of Larry Itliong.

I was going inside the hall one day when at the entrance a Filipino and a Mexican were talking to each other. It was a narrow entrance so I asked permission to pass between them. After I passed a few steps by them, I heard a soft voice say, "Hello, brother!" I looked back and I answered, "Hello, brother!"

When I walked back to shake his hand, I learned that the Mexican man was Cesar. I felt very impressed and honored that Cesar called me brother. Ever since that time we called each other brother.

I remember in April, 1969, Cesar called me in Oakland where I was working for the union and said, "I want you to leave your job as a fund-raiser. Let Candido Feliciano take charge of your business there. I want you to come and take charge of the barbecue for the representational election of the farmworkers in Coachella."

In May, 1969, he appointed me to direct the Coachella Valley grape strike. I said to Cesar, "Please send all the Filipinos and Mexicans you can spare."

He did. Our strike force was so strong the bosses told their workers, "Pick only the cream of the crop." After the harvest, there were thousands of yellow bunches of grapes left hanging on the vines. The strike was a success. I remember Cesar told me, "Peter, pack your things and come home to Delano."

It was after the Coachella strike that Cesar approached me and said, "Brother, we are broke. Go back again to raise funds in Oakland." After one week in Oakland, he called me and said, "Peter, I want you to pack your things and come home to Delano."

I questioned his request. "Hey brother! What is up?" I asked. "You just sent me here a week ago. Why are you asking me to come home?"

He answered, "Because I want you to be a national fund-raiser."

I repeated what he said. "National fund-raiser? I don't think I like it. It is too big for me to handle."

"Pack your things. Come home tomorrow," he ordered. I said to him, "OK. I will accept your proposal on one condition."

He asked, "What is that?"

I replied, "On the condition that the Bay Area is my headquarters." I hate failure. In the Bay Area I was already established.

He said, "No Peter, Delano will be your headquarters. Pack your things and come home." His tone was final. He had plans for bigger fund-raisers.

In 1971, Cesar appointed me to take Larry Itliong's unexpired term on the National Executive Board.

"Do you want to take it?" he asked.

"Yes sir. I'll take it with great honor," I replied.

In September, 1971, Cesar said, "I want you to go to Stockton and head the field office there." We had a few

Riding the wind to freedom.

contracts there. It was my job to enforce the contracts and report any violations that the workers reported to me. It was a pleasure to serve the needs of the farmworkers there.

I remember the combined concern of Cesar and Larry about the elderly Filipinos who were soon to retire. The Filipinos didn't have homes or families. The Executive Board approved their proposal to build a home for the retirees. It was inaugurated in 1972, and Tom Donahue, secretary of the AFL-CIO, was our guest speaker. It was named in honor of Paulo Agbayani, a Filipino striker who died of heatstroke under the hot sun on the picket line.

On January 10, 1974, Cesar sent me to direct the boycott of iceberg lettuce and Gallo wine in Baltimore, Maryland. Before I left for Baltimore, I asked Cesar, "What is your advice?" He said, "Organize the churches and you've got it made."

I delegated the churches to John Proctor, a former director of religious education. He was a volunteer. I believe I gave him his cup of tea when I appointed him to organize the churches. Like Cesar told me to do, the churches were organized.

While in Baltimore, Cesar was my guest speaker twice, once in a college stadium and the other time at the College of Notre Dame. The famous farmworkers movie, *Fighting for Our Lives*, was sent to me and to many other boycott offices to raise funds for *La Causa*.

One day Cesar called me and said, "Peter! When are you going to show *Fighting for Our Lives*?" I replied, "I am still in gear but no date set as yet.

He said, "In Hollywood Jim Drake is charging $100 a plate for dinner and the showing of the movie."

"A $100-a-plate dinner?" I repeated.

"Yes. He just called me today," he replied.

I felt like the goat in me was being challenged, so I said, "Hell! If Jim Drake can charge $100 a plate, so can I."

Wow! Can you imagine how he took my reply? I bet you he was laughing to himself after I hung up the phone. Laughing at how his message got me obligated to do fund-raising.

Well it was no problem. "I am a man of my word," I thought to myself. "All I can do is try my best."

I was in luck. I found a lovely nun volunteer in a convent in Catonsville. I designated her as co-chairperson to organize and promote the $100-a-plate dinner and showing of *Fighting for Our Lives*. I told her to organize the churches and I would organize the AFL-CIO Central Labor Councils and others. She got the College of Notre Dame to donate the dining room and auditorium for the showing of the movie.

We grossed about $7,000. We were very grateful and happy. Priests, nuns, labor representatives and others were present to meet with Cesar.

And do you know what? That lovely nun is now my wife. You don't think I'd let a good organizer and lovely woman go do you?

I also remember Cesar, on August 27, 1977, at the party at the Fresno Selland Arena after the election. Cesar and I were drinking and dancing together with glasses of union wine—either Paul Mason, Almaden or Christian Brothers—in our hands and we were singing as we danced. Helen and my wife Dolores were laughing at us. They, too, were enjoying their glasses of wine.

I had been reelected third vice president by acclamation and Cesar continued on as our president by acclamation under the UFW AFL-CIO. There was good reason for drinking and dancing together to celebrate.

I remember Cesar as loving to children. I saw him talking to many children in a caring and compassionate way. His grandson Robert was together with him in a poster.

I also remember Cesar as lover to animals like his dogs Boycott and Huelga. He also provided water for birds and foxes in the back of Nan Freeman Hall.

I remember Cesar as a sports lover. He asked his son Birdie (Anthony Chavez) to prepare the TV at the conference room. He invited football enthusiasts, especially those whose teams were different from his own team.

I remember Cesar talked about his victory in playing

handball with his bodyguards on their way to his speaking engagements.

I also remember Cesar designating a Saturday when field organizers visited La Paz for.a meeting with softball and barbecue afterwards. I remember him as a permanent pitcher of his team. He pitched softly, especially to little ball players.

I also remember myself hollering, "Change the pitcher! Change the pitcher!" when someone would hit a home run.

I remember Cesar had a shy and magnetic smile.

I remember Cesar when he called a community meeting. Everybody was on time. When he came in there was an atmosphere of complete silence and reverence. One could almost hear a pin drop. There was something about him that enchanted people. It is hard to describe it. Perhaps they call it charisma. To put it in my own words, he was out of this world. He was different from other people.

I also remember when I called his office, most of the time he was not in. He was out almost every day on speaking engagements. He never sat long enough to keep his chair warm.

I remember Cesar always did his homework when he called a board meeting. He was always prepared to give his plans and ideas for the farmworkers.

One day while I was in his office, I said, "Gosh! You have lots of new books."

"Peter," he said, "If you don't read new books, you are left behind. I spend time reading into the night. I want to be ahead of others."

Brother Cesar was, to me, the greatest farmworker leader, teacher and fearless fighter for the rights and justice for the poorest of the poor—my brother and sister farmworkers.

He taught us how to walk in the jungle. He taught us not to be afraid to fight—nonviolently—for our rights, dignity, self-respect and to respect the rights of others. He is God's gift to the farmworkers and to people in all walks of life. He has left us this legacy so that the struggle will continue on with our lives, and we will teach our children about his life so that they will know they are first-class citizens like Cesar wanted us to be.

He is my hero and my brother. I feel elated to have given twenty-eight years of my life as a volunteer of service to the cause of the farmworkers side-by-side with him.

Peter Gines Velasco was among 1,500 Filipinos who struck the Delano grape growers under AWOC September 8, 1965. On December 12, 1975, he married Dolores Neubauer in Agbayani Village. He served on the UFW executive board from 1971 to 1988. In October, 1988, Cesar Chavez and the board members awarded him the title of secretary-treasurer, emeritus.

Heads and hearts embrace.

"Our lives are all that truly belong to us...only by giving our lives do we find life. I am convinced that the truest act of courage...is to sacrifice ourselves for others in a totally nonviolent struggle for justice."

With these words Cesar Chavez ended his twenty-five day fast in 1968. His words are as relevant today as they were then.

It was through Cesar's efforts and those of the UFW that the country came to understand the plight of the farmworker and the onerous and, at times, dehumanizing and dangerous working conditions of the farm laborer.

Cesar's life was dedicated to the same basic principles found at the heart of Catholic social thought: the affirmation of human life and dignity; the defense of human rights; the promotion of the right to work and the right to organize to secure decent working conditions and wages; and an unwavering solidarity with and option for the poor.

In Lent of 1966, Cesar led a march to the California state capitol to petition the governor to secure collective bargaining rights for farmworkers. On Wednesday of Holy Week, the marchers celebrated the news that the first major grower had agreed to recognize the union and negotiate a labor contract. On Holy Thursday, a second grower agreed to hold union elections. At noon on Easter Sunday, ten thousand people gathered on the capitol steps and adjacent lawns to pray and pledge continued support for the farmworkers' cause.

Cesar's message to the workers that day was clear and succinct: You have the right to organize and negotiate for just wages and working conditions. The message to the growers, while less obvious, was equally eloquent: You are successful enough to earn a profit and still treat your employees with justice. And he proved to both groups that this could be accomplished without violence and without diminishing anyone's rights or dignity.

When violence was used to intimidate workers, Cesar would resort to the nonviolent weapons of prayer and fasting to confront his opponents. He refused, to the end, to engage in violence or to allow others to do so in the name of the UFW.

I believe it is right and fitting to honor the values which guided Cesar's life: the right to work; the need to stand on the side of the most vulnerable; the principle of empowerment; and the dignity of the human person.

Every person has the right to work and should have the opportunity to secure for himself and his family the basic things that make life dignified. It is the duty of us all to work to ensure that public policy upholds and protects those rights.

Cardinal Roger Mahony is with the Archdiocese of Los Angeles.

The gathering storm.

I claim my dignity, my power.

"I'm still trying to get someone interested in being crazy enough to give up eating and join me to develop the newspaper." —Cesar Chavez, July 26, 1963. Upon arriving in March, 1972, at the United Farm Workers headquarters in La Paz, I was assigned to work as a typesetter/reporter on the union's newspaper, *El Malcriado*.

Cesar Chavez was preoccupied in 1972 with organizing the United Farm Workers as a national union since it had just received its charter from the AFL-CIO. That was also the year he declared an international lettuce boycott and on May 12, he started a twenty-four day fast in protest against Arizona's anti-farmworker law.

Despite his busy schedule, he stopped by *El Malcriado*'s office unexpectedly one late summer afternoon. My concentration was interrupted by the swift entry of Cesar's two faithful companions Boycott and Huelga, two large German shepherds whose appearance always announced their master's presence. Cesar was concerned about the newspaper's contents. He told the staff, "I remember when the old *El Malcriado* was too controversial. The growers hated it. We were being sued. We need to meet the fine line between being controversial and too controversial."

Cesar criticized the recent editions as "blah, no spirit, no fire, no life!" He urged, "It's got to be controversial. Workers should love it or hate it!"

On a quiet New Year's Day in 1973, I had an opportunity to ask Cesar about the beginnings of the farmworkers' newspaper. He explained, "I had the idea...I felt an instrument of communication needed to belong to the workers. We needed it to print the internal work of the organization. I knew we could not rely on the public press to do it."

He continued, "Newspapers play major roles in all struggles." He admitted he was influenced by Hindu reformer Mahatma Gandhi who established and worked closely with his own newspaper.

Cesar remembered reading about a little newspaper printed during the Mexican revolution called *Malcriado*, meaning a person who is rude, uncivil, outspoken, because the paper was dangerously speaking out against the power structure.

He explained, "I choose the name *El Malcriado* because the growers have a paternalistic attitude toward their workers. The name *Malcriado* fits well because the growers are paternal and the newspaper is talking back to them like a child talking back to his father."

The newspaper's name was a play on words. He said, "The name is satirical, rather than call it the plow, hoe or tractor." Hence, *El Malcriado* was born with its subtitle, *The Voice of the Farm Worker*.

From the very beginning with the first Spanish edition published in December, 1964, Cesar's idea for the fledgling newspaper was "to get our side across to the farmworker." He explained, "I saw the paper as a propaganda tool, a way of educating the membership, to stimulate the farmworkers to action and to hit the opposition hard and get the members to react."

The paper's first task: to challenge the powerful agricultural structure in California's Central Valley coupled with the small paper's economic struggle to survive against angry storeowner distributors and an indifferent public.

Cesar sighed as he recalled the struggle, "The early editions were not effective. People wouldn't even take them for free. We had to sell and build up *El Malcriado*. It was a new thing and it took a long time to get the idea across."

In August, 1965, the first English edition appeared for the benefit of those farmworkers who did not read Spanish and the predominately English-reading supporters.

Cesar said, "The English edition never made a direct appeal to the worker. It appealed more to the city people, the supporters. The Spanish editions were more effective with the farmworkers. It wasn't meant to be; it just happened that way."

On the afternoon of our discussion about the newspaper, Cesar thought for a moment and described the 1972 editions, "In terms of education, *El Malcriado* is more effective. In terms of propaganda, it is less effective."

When asked about the newspaper's effectiveness as an organizing tool, Cesar replied, "It's hard to judge. It's one of the many things we use to organize with. In that context, it's been effective."

Cesar agreed with me when I defined *El Malcriado* as an important medium extending the limited means available to the farmworkers to communicate their hopes and needs to a wider public.

Elaine Flora Graves worked in a variety of jobs while at La Paz from 1972 to 1976, including six months on the Denver boycott.

4:00 A.M.—pushing our way to work.

When I was in high school and working in the fields, we were not allowed to drink water nor did we have toilets. Cesar fought for humanity and he made things change.

I benefited by Cesar's struggles to make sure that farmworkers would no longer be treated like animals. This had a significant impact on me because it made me realize that a person or a small group *can* make a difference. It was beyond my imagination that such significant changes would ever materialize.

As I grow older, I always think back to what Cesar's struggles were all about. His struggles have driven me to become involved with my community. Cesar made me believe that nothing is impossible.

Dolores Gallegos is a former farmworker who was fired for drinking water. She went on to become a school teacher in Hanford, California and was recently elected to the Hanford City Council.

*I am a sacred life
rising above this poverty.*

Cesar Chavez was not an ordinary man. He organized the first truly effective union for farmworkers, but what was more significant was that he set an example of a way of life based on sharing and frugality. He went against the grain by living simply despite his fame.

His union dramatically lifted the wages of farmworkers and improved their conditions—successes nowhere else attained. Yet Chavez, to the end, continued to seek more than traditional trade union goals.

What he wanted was a form of human empowerment that would make possible a truly good life based on cooperative forms of ownership. He talked to me often of the limitations of collective bargaining and liberal politics as they are practiced now.

The first time I met Cesar Chavez was in 1966 when he visited my father's house in Los Angeles. Everyone else had on suits and ties. Chavez wore simple work clothes. I noticed how small he was and how quiet and unassuming.

I sensed a person totally different from the others in the room. This was a campaign year when Ronald Reagan was running against my father, Pat Brown. The people who came and went were persons of power and ambition. Chavez seemed different. You knew he was representing a cause much greater than himself.

I saw Chavez again on a farmworker march to Calexico and then when I sought his union's endorsement for my gubernatorial campaign in 1974. My first visit to La Paz, his rural headquarters east of Bakersfield, is still vivid in my mind. The place was totally off the beaten path, yet there were hundreds of people around—mostly young and with infectious vitality and enthusiasm. It was clear that the United Farm Workers was a movement. Nuns were typing in the outer office, herb tea was served along with the vegetarian food in the common dining room, young volunteers went about their work with a sense of mission. Frankly, I was drawn to it.

The critics kept repeating that Chavez had to form a real union that knew how to get along with management and service collective bargaining contracts. True enough, but from my point of view, the UFW was on the forefront of working for genuine social change—not merely its illusion—and that required precisely the dedication and sacrifice which Chavez inspired.

My real work with Chavez began shortly after my election as governor when we met in my home in Los Angeles to talk about a proposed farm labor bill. Chavez pulled up to my Laurel Canyon house in an old car with a German shepherd dog named Huelga—Spanish for "strike."

We talked for several hours about whether the proposed state law or any labor law could actually help farmworkers. Chavez repeatedly said that his boycott was a much better organizing tool because the law would always be captured by the powerful economic interests that control politics. I argued with him and said that a law would be his best protection. He finally agreed, but remained skeptical.

A few months later, the historic California Labor Relations Act was passed in special session. Hundreds of elections were then conducted, most of which the UFW won in competition with the Teamsters. Yet, by the next year the growers succeeded in blocking all funding for the act and proved Chavez correct that a mere law could not overcome the bitter opposition and incredible political power of agribusiness.

During the last few months of his life, Chavez and I met twice—once in La Paz and once in my house in San Francisco. When we met in La Paz, we attended Mass and then ate breakfast in the cafeteria-style dining room. While we were eating, he remarked that he had a hard time getting some of his own family to eat together in the big dining room.

This was something he felt strongly. For Chavez, some form of common life was the most natural way for human beings to live.

In our last conversation, Chavez made very clear that he

We have to be carefully taught.

My voice swells to freedom.

believed that some type of producer cooperative was the next step for working people because individuals had to have ownership and a real stake in what they did. He told me that it was his goal to get land and develop a cooperative.

Cesar Chavez was a man who transcended the opinions and passing certitudes of the day. He had an overwhelming sense that modern life was disordered and that human beings were being cut off from the soil and a harmonious balance of friendship and nature. He recoiled from the pervasive waste and poisoning that we call our affluent modern life.

Cesar Chavez ended his life as he began it, close to those who toil with their hands. In a mechanical age full of plastic and loneliness, he stood against the crowd, unbossed, undoctored and unbought. He kept the faith to the end. We won't find another like him.

Jerry Brown, formerly the governor of California, was elected mayor of Oakland in 1998.

I'd like to share a personal story that underscores the depth of Cesar Chavez's belief in people. This is my own version of *Stand and Deliver*.

In 1975, with the enactment of the California Agricultural Labor Relations Act, the United Farm Workers won the majority of farm representation elections. Those election victories left the UFW with a shortage of union negotiators and field office administrators. Cesar was under pressure to recruit and hire professionals to negotiate contracts and represent employees.

But the union comprised more than 100,000 low-wage workers, and Cesar didn't want the job of negotiating and administering contracts to go exclusively to college-educated professionals. Cesar decided to select and train twelve young people in a comprehensive negotiation/education program. He picked me and his son Paul for two of the slots. Among the others he selected were a high school dropout turned printer, a recovering substance abuser, four farmworkers without high school diplomas, a former nun, three grape boycott organizers and a button maker who had dropped out of high school.

Some of those chosen didn't speak English. They had to learn. No one would have considered us qualified candidates to be union negotiators, negotiators who would be required to oppose some of the top management consulting firms and top law firms in the country.

The negotiating school's instruction was intense. We studied English and Spanish, math, economics and union organizing. We learned about labor law, bad-faith bargaining, union rights to organize and economic action. This was the preliminary course work.

Then we studied the practice of managing and negotiating contracts. We were taught how to organize, train, and manage bargaining committees. We were taught how to get the membership to actively participate in the process.

The schedule was a ten-hour day, six days a week for twelve months. It was an enormous commitment by the union. The results over the next four years proved worth the effort. We were able to negotiate the first cost-of-living allowances in the history of agriculture, improvements in medical and pension plans, and the hiring of full-time union representatives paid by those ranches needing a strong union presence.

Today, the button maker has a law degree. The former substance abuser is vice president of a city-employee local union in the San Francisco Bay Area. One of the boycott organizers completed college and works for the National Aeronautics and Space Administration in New Mexico, while another is the president of his local union in Michigan. One of the farmworkers currently administers the UFW's medical plan in Mexico. Another has become a well-known political organizer in San Diego. A third is an international representative for the United Food and Commercial Workers Union. A fourth directs a vocational training program in Riverside County, California. Cesar's son Paul is the executive

"God is my life."
God guides our
family as we travel
the Texas-California loop.

¡Sí! ¡Sí se puede!

officer for the movement's nonprofit entities, valued at more than $10 million.

I left the UFW in 1984 and graduated from college in 1987. I was hired by Massachusetts Governor Michael Dukakis to direct four states for his presidential campaign in 1988. We were victorious in all of them.

Cesar had faith in us. Today, you hear a lot about the word, "empowerment." Cesar believed that if you give workers a chance, provide real support, help them build their self-confidence, and heap plenty of recognition and encouragement for little victories, they will rise to meet the challenge of even the highest standards.

Thank you Cesar.

David Villarino, Cesar's son-in-law, was a labor relations representative for the California State Employees Association and later became director of the UFW's collective bargaining department.

Traveling a mighty hard life.

I t was the infamous summer of 1973. The grape strike had begun in the Coachella Valley after the growers had dumped all the United Farm Workers contracts that had been signed in 1970.

I was in Arizona working the boycott. The United Church of Christ was preparing to go into its biannual General Synod meeting in St. Louis the weekend of June 23 and 24.

I got the word through Chris Hartmire that Cesar wanted me to go to the General Synod meeting and get strong support from the UCC for the strikers. When I arrived in St. Louis, I met John Moyer who was a board member of the National Farm Workers Ministry and a staff person for the UCC Board of Homeland Ministries. Together we sat down and mapped out a strategy to get a resolution passed supporting the grape strike.

In the meantime, after checking back with the UFW headquarters at La Paz, I found out that what Cesar really wanted was for a planeload of church people to fly out to California to personally witness the violence being waged against the farmworkers. He might as well want the moon, I thought. But Cesar knew that you don't get what you don't ask for, and, I decided, church folks might just think this was important enough to do.

Of course Cesar was right. Somehow, the spirit began to move. When we explained the situation to our supporters, they became very excited at the possibility of doing something bold and important. Work began on lining up delegate support so that when the issue hit the floor of the Synod there would be support for a vote to stand with the farmworkers in their hour of need. The vote was taken and the measure passed. A planeload of delegates from the General Synod representing the United Church of Christ would be sent.

My father, the Reverend Reuben P. Koehler, was conference minister for the Missouri Conference at the time and was attending the synod meeting. As soon as it became clear that our plan might work, he stayed up in his hotel room and began calling airlines to charter a flight to San Bernadino, California. It looked rather bleak for a while, until he found a Pan Am flight that was headed to St. Louis from India which would be available.

That night, Monday, June 25, 1973, ninety-five delegates, me included, boarded the Pan Am jet for California. We flew all night and landed just as the sun was coming up. We then got on a bus and drove east to Indio and then into the Coachella Valley. As we got close to Coachella, we observed a group of rather large men who had gathered in the parking lot of a Safeway grocery store. They were the "goon squads" brought in by the growers to beat and intimidate the farmworkers and their families.

When we got to the UFW office, we saw hundreds of farmworkers gathering in the park waiting for Cesar to lead the morning meeting. Cesar met us at the park. He introduced us to the gathered farmworkers who cheered and welcomed us. We then went out in a caravan of ten or twelve carloads of people to the picket lines in the fields. We later found out why it was important to travel in a caravan.

That afternoon we saw a family of farmworkers that had gotten separated from the group. They were run off the road by some of the goon squad, and three were beaten until they had no teeth left.

Later in the day, after encountering the goon squad terrorists on the picket lines, we gathered around the remains of a young family's home that had been burnt to the ground the night before. The family escaped without harm, but they were pretty frightened. The husband was one of the strike leaders. We not only prayed for the family and the farmworkers, we also celebrated communion using grapes from Lionel Steinberg, the only UFW label left in the valley.

It was exactly twenty-four hours later when we touched down again in St. Louis. We were tired, dirty and hot. But we were also filled with a sense of purpose. If our faith was to mean anything, then we had to put it to work pursuing justice. The delegation arrived back at the synod meeting, which was continuing. The door burst open at the convention center, and the delegates paraded through the aisles, bringing everyone a taste of the UFW-picked grapes. All of a sudden, a booming voice came over the loud speaker, "Brothers and sisters of the United Church of Christ. You should know how much your witness has meant to the farmworkers and their families in their pursuit of justice. We thank you." A speakerphone had been hooked up to the P.A. system so that Cesar could address the convention. Cesar's voice sounded like the voice of God speaking to the chosen ones.

We later learned that the delegation was the top story on both the AP and UPI wires that morning—until 10:00 A.M. that was. At 10:00 A.M. John Dean took the stand for the first time in the impeachment hearings on President Nixon.

Short as this coverage was, the delegation's visit—instigated by Cesar's bold request—helped to trigger the national spotlight on the plight of the farmworkers and the violence they were forced to endure. As more and more national attention was drawn to the Coachella Valley, the goon squads were called off. Unfortunately, it was not the end of the violence. As the strike moved north, the Kern County Sheriff's Department soon took over where the goon squads left off.

Many staff and supporters were quite concerned for Cesar's safety that summer. He would go out and visit picket lines every day. I remember Cesar telling us, "They want us to strike back in violence. If we do that, then we're defeated." Cesar believed his presence was essential to keep that from happening.

David M. Koehler worked as a staff member for the National Farm Worker Ministry for more than six years, working for Cesar Chavez and the United Farm Workers of America, AFL-CIO, primarily in the grape and lettuce boycotts.

Dancing with the rhythms of life.

I got a frantic call at about 9:30 A.M. from a *campesina* who lived in Cabrillo Village—a farm labor camp on the outskirts of Oxnard. The camp was owned by citrus growers and the farmworkers who lived in the camp were some of the strongest pro-UFW workers in California. The harvest season was ending and many of the workers were packing up to move north with the harvest. To intimidate the remaining workers, every time a family moved out of a house, the company ordered the house destroyed.

On this particular day, a family had moved out and just as quickly a bulldozer arrived to level the simple wooden frame house.

"What do we do? What do we do?" the *campesina* screamed in the phone.

My stomach churned; my head throbbed. "What would Cesar do?" I thought.

"Surround the house," I yelled over the phone. "Get every child, every person in the camp to surround the house. You must stop the bulldozer. I'll be there as quickly as I can."

As soon as I hung up, I called La Paz trying to get hold of Cesar. As luck would have it, he was in Calexico and in those days we had no cell phones or pagers. I told Esther, Cesar's secretary, I needed to talk to Cesar immediately. I had a crisis that needed his attention.

When I arrived at the labor camp about twenty minutes later, the women and children (the men were at work) had completely surrounded the house and were singing, "*No nos moveran*" (we will not be moved). The bulldozer driver was bewildered. "Hey, man, I don't want no trouble. I don't want to do this." The police and the foreman of the camp arrived about the same time I did. The foreman was about to explode. His face was as red as an overripe beet.

The police, to their credit, decided they would do nothing. This was, in fact, the farmworkers' camp. They were

not trespassing. We were deadlocked. The farmworkers were singing; the foreman was ranting. After about twenty minutes of intense standoff, the tension was broken by the bulldozer driver starting his engine and driving away. We had won temporarily.

That night I spoke to Cesar. He said he would drive up and meet with workers the next evening in the camp. My job was to get them there. The next evening Cesar arrived. He said the only solution to the problem would be to have the workers buy the camp. "What?" I thought, but said nothing.

That evening I watched in stunned silence as groups of workers, ten to fifteen at a time, came into the house to meet with Cesar. His style was incredible. He told stories of other workers. He told them their biggest problem was their own fear and that unless they made a commitment to themselves and to their families to fight, they would always be kicked out of somewhere. They needed to take a stand, if not now, someday when they had overcome their fear.

It was clear to him that this was the time to make a stand, but he didn't tell them what to do. He let them make their own decisions. He did this not by fancy rhetoric or impassioned speeches, but by looking at people in their eyes, by talking softly and clearly, and by making them laugh. The laughter was the first step in overcoming the fear.

By the time the meetings ended, very late at night, Cesar had talked to every family in the camp. Only a few decided to move out. Everyone else decided that they would do whatever was necessary to save the camp and save the houses.

Three years later the workers achieved their goal. Through a state grant, funds were set aside to allow the workers to purchase the camp and develop a community housing cooperative.

Ten years later I was speaking to a young man at Stanford University. He informed me he was the son of a migrant farmworker who attended those meetings with Cesar that night. His family decided to stay and fight. Their home—the labor camp—was the first permanent home they had. He was able to attend local schools, the local community college and then eventually transfer to Stanford. His words were, "Cesar changed my life that night. I will always be grateful."

From 1971 to 1982, Larry Tramutola worked with the UFW. In 1993, he trained electoral organizers in South Africa in preparation for their first free democratic election.

My son knows who I am.

In the summer of 1973, in the sweltering heat of the Coachella Valley, I met with Cesar Chavez for a few minutes in the United Farm Workers' office next to Westerfield Park, just like hundreds of farmworkers with whom he held afternoon counsel.

It was a violent summer. Although I spent no more than two days there, I never forgot standing in the early morning picket line in the Riverside County countryside across from the Teamster goons in the midst of sheriff riot squads.

The lessons of risk and political sacrifice for farmworker dignity seemed so clear then. The lessons have proven indelible as time has passed. Perhaps to honor and thank the teacher, perhaps to preserve the historical moment, I joined the more than 30,000 marchers in Delano on April 29, 1993. I know there were, among the thousands, many who had been taught these and many more moral political lessons.

For my generation of California Chicanos—both urban and rural—the farmworker struggle was our civil rights movement. "Viva *La Causa*" was a struggle slogan of pride and rage. Racism was real at the local supermarket picket line. The streets were for marches of protest. Social movements were not things of fiction and history. There was meaning to life larger than your own well-being and future.

Of course, the farmworker vision of a better life was best put before Californians in the 1960s and 1970s by the UFW strikes and boycotts. Advocacy groups like the California Rural Legal Assistance took the example and integrated the union's objectives into their social change agendas. Equally significant was Chavez' inspiration, leaving in its wake a legacy of justice advocates whom he motivated to address the plight of the farmworkers and others.

I, for one, was moved to attend law school with the single purpose of using these legal skills in rural California, where I had been born and raised. My legal ambition was simple—to put my lawyering in the hands of either the CRLA or the UFW and change the lives of farmworkers and poor folk for the better. My two days on the picket line had changed my life direction forever.

The Coachella lesson about violence and risk happened for me about twenty-five years ago. Because of it, I have yet to feel grief over the loss of Cesar Chavez. The funeral was celebratory for me—a communal farewell to an extraordinary man who believed that the farm laborer not only had the right to sit at the negotiation table with the grower, but that farmworkers had the human right to a just wage and benefits that might keep their families out of poverty.

In pursuit of that unionization vision, Cesar irreversibly gave faith to thousands of farmworkers who came to believe in this simple cause. That vision, in our lifetimes, taught American labor that the field worker was organizable and entitled to labor law protection equal to that of other laborers. Neither society nor farmworkers will ever be the same.

Thank you, *companero*, for the political lessons, the justice, vision and life direction. May your soul rest in peace. May we continue your fight.

Jose Padilla, executive director of the California Rural Legal Assistance

Single-hearted.

That's what I remember most about Cesar.

Like most Christians, I have never had much trouble understanding most of the Beatitudes, the series of "blesseds" Jesus proclaimed to a large crowd in his Sermon on the Mount. But I never was quite able to grasp what Jesus meant in one of the Beatitudes when he used the original word for what some scripture scholars have translated as "single-hearted": "Blessed are the single-hearted, for they shall see God."

I understand the word better now. Cesar defined it for me.

In the twelve years I spent at La Paz, the 100-acre site of the United Farm Workers's headquarters/community near Bakersfield, I was in constant awe of Cesar's indefatigable zeal for the single cause of making life fairer and better for migrant farmworkers. For him, everything else was peripheral.

However, being single-hearted, even in such noble causes as peace, nonviolence and justice for all, does not insure that the person who fits that description is automatically going to be universally admired and appreciated. Such utterly focused people can cause chagrin and discomfort among companions and coworkers who are less relentless about and less dedicated to the task at hand. Gandhi was not easy to work or live with. Neither was Dorothy Day. And neither was Cesar Chavez.

But because Cesar was unflagging in his efforts for migrant farmworkers—endlessly organizing, marching, boycotting, speaking, lobbying, praying—life for migrant farmworkers in the United States is better than ever before. Because Cesar did what everybody said was impossible—that is, organize migrant farmworkers into a union—life for migrant farmworkers not only did get better but will continue to get better because of Cesar's primary legacy, the United Farm Workers of America.

Cesar probably will never be declared a saint. He was, like most of us, too flawed for that. However, no one can deny that, in the interest of a noble cause, he was utterly single-hearted. Along with remembering that, we remember also that Jesus promised the single-hearted that they would see God.

For Cesar, I'm sure that promise has already been fulfilled. Even if Cesar is never declared a saint, seeing God isn't exactly small potatoes.

We should be so lucky!

Father Ken Irrgang was ordained a priest in 1968. He lived and worked at La Paz from 1977 to 1989.

God's spirit is in us.

ANN MCGREGOR

I knew Cesar best as social worker. I had been assigned to help reactivate the service centers (called campesino centers) for farmworkers and their families following the grape contract victories in the early 1970s. These centers were a network of facilities operating in rural areas wherever the union had contracts. Designed to teach farmworkers how to survive in an atmosphere hostile to the very people putting food on the American table, the centers were of special interest to Cesar. It was his philosophy of service, unique in every aspect, that built the United Farm Workers Union.

I soon learned that the campesino centers would not charge for their services. Instead, the farmworker would be asked to help the union, and others with a similar problem, in return for the union's help to him. We called this the "service exchange" or "trade-off." It was negotiated at the outset and was very effective in building a strong union and making a strong worker capable of solving his own problems.

I learned, too, that the centers were not information and referral agencies. Staff, all volunteer, would accompany the worker to the agency where assistance was available. En route, the worker would be taught about the benefit for which he was applying, how he qualified and how to secure this benefit. This system ensured that the applicant got to the right destination and was not talked out of his right to an economic or other benefit. It also ensured that the worker knew that it was his union that was helping him.

Cesar explained to us and to campesino center staff that it is important to teach the worker how to complete applications and other forms himself, to learn to do his own tax returns and even his own appeals. If we didn't do this, we weren't really helping him at all. This was part of the excitement in our campesino center program. Classes on income tax return preparation were held wherever there were centers. The worker then, in turn, taught his brother-in-law or neighbor to do his own returns. This "each-one-teach-one"

principle applied to all areas of assistance: unemployment insurance, labor law enforcement, workers' compensation, etc.

Another fundamental we learned from Cesar was follow-through. This meant to keep checking and working on a case until a satisfactory conclusion was reached. Lessons from Cesar also included how to greet the person entering the center so that he felt welcome and immediately knew that he had come to the right place. We were taught to demand bilingual forms from agencies and to demand that every courtesy and consideration be afforded to farmworkers of differing races and languages.

Instructions on recruiting staff volunteers specified not to overlook the elderly and disabled. First and foremost, Cesar said, we should recruit the individual with what he called "heart." Academic background and experience were not necessary. The mark of a good center, we were told, was the one swarming with volunteers.

Our centers were effective. We were effective. We had a teacher who developed strengths, ability and talents we didn't know we had. Cesar was a natural social worker who made those of us who worked with him his surrogates, and we, in turn, made social workers and loyal union members out of those we helped.

The lessons we learned from Cesar were lessons from his heart. That heart lives on.

Ann McGregor retired in 1988 as executive director of the Martin Luther King, Jr. Farm Workers' Fund. On staff with the union for seventeen years, she was named a national representative of the UFW in 1986.

"If to build our union required the deliberate taking of life, either the life of a grower or his child, or the life of a farmworker or his child, then I choose not to see the union built."
—Cesar Chavez

After many years of negotiating and organizing in Mexico, finally, in 1965 the stage was set for the inauguration of the United States-Mexico Automotive Coordinating Council. I was proud of our collective effort with the Geneva based International Metalworkers' Federation. The fiery American labor leader Walter Reuther was both the United Auto Workers' president and chairman of the IMF World Auto Council and he would travel to Mexico to address and inaugurate the powerful new body that would unite United States and Mexican autoworkers together in a giant North-American union. This was the long sought collective bargaining dream of the UAW, although a nightmare to the giant automakers of Detroit.

I began to draw up the list of trade union dignitaries from both sides of the border invited to this historic event. Joining Walter would be his brother Victor who was UAW's International Affairs chief. Other associates would complete the circle, Jack Conway, Henry Santiestevan, UAW Western Region Director Paul Schrade, Hank Lacayo and others. Paul Schrade, a close supporter of Cesar Chavez, suggested Cesar be placed on the list in order to introduce Cesar to the Mexican labor movement and to build labor solidarity for the farmworkers. Cesar's wife, Helen, and my wife, Arcy, would join the group.

Reuther's dramatic and resounding call for United States-Mexico unity among autoworkers carried the day. The Mexican labor leaders and rank and file members roared approval as waves of shouts gave way to the ribbon cutting ceremonies of the new Automotive Council's headquarters in Mexico City. Our mission had been a success and labor historians would recount this day.

Cesar had never been to Mexico City, so I arranged for us to take a tour outside the city to visit the famous city of the Aztec pyramids at Teotihuacán. Our wives joined us. We hailed a tourist taxi and asked the driver to proceed to the pyramids. After about an hour's drive we caught a glimpse of the towering Pyramid of the Sun looming ahead. It was a spectacular sight. I saw Cesar and Helen hold their breath.

Then, at that moment, the taxi driver slowed up and made a sharp turn off the highway onto a bumpy dirt road where he proceeded for about fifty yards and came to a stop. To the right of the car was a large pile of rubble and dirt debris. He then said for us to get out and dig around the rubble. He said he would return for us in about thirty minutes, claiming that these were excellent excavation grounds. Since we hadn't paid him we were not afraid of being abandoned, so we proceeded to dig.

Sure enough Cesar was the first to cry out, "Look, I found an arm." He was elated and soon all of us were uncovering bits of pre-Columbian artifacts, pottery parts and a number of beads. We were no longer unionists but rather fledging archaeologists thrown into a treasure trove. Finally the driver returned and cut our frenzy short.

We went on to visit the giant Pyramid of the Sun, having left our proud possessions in the care of the taxi driver. The tour was ever so much more complete knowing that as we scaled the steps of the stone temple we had mementos of our proud culture.

We returned to our hotel and rewarded the driver with an appropriate tip for providing us an excellent tour and exposure to Aztec antiquities.

Meeting up again with our Mexican union brothers, Cesar could not contain himself and put forth his find and said, "Look at my collection. But is it legal for me to take them home?" They looked at him and said, "Oh, it's all right. You should know that it's rumored that the drivers plant these out there for the benefit of the American tourists."

Many years later, when I visited Cesar in La Paz, he pulled a small plastic bag out of his desk and said to me, "Remember these? They really are a part of our past."

I agreed. To this day, I still have mine.

In March of 1998, Esteban Edward Torres, after a sixteen-year career in the House of Representatives, marked by his unabashed commitment to American workers, announced his retirement from Congress.

Determination knows no age.

I knew Cesar Chavez existed long before I met him. Our paths were bound to cross. I, along with tens of thousands of others, gravitated toward this man's inexplicable magnetism.

The first time I saw Cesar was from a distance. Hundreds of farmworkers and the curious, like myself, had gathered at El Teatro Azteca in Fresno. We were there to hear why farmworkers had made the decision to march more than 300 miles from the city of Delano to Sacramento, the state capital.

The marchers limped into the theatre. I watched as a young man, not of huge size, limped up onto the stage bracing himself with a cane.

This was Cesar Chavez.

When he started to speak, the noisy, cheering crowd came to an instant silence. In later years, I noted time and again that when Cesar got up to speak, the din died down, as if on cue, as if an instant sedative had been given to the audience. One could hear the proverbial pin.

When he finished speaking, he would be surrounded with people. They had to touch him, speak to him, reveal their particular sorrows. Cesar would listen, give advice. He never turned away and said, "Not now, I'm too busy," "See my secretary," "Send me a memo," or issued similar rejections. He knew everybody's name, what ranch they worked on or had walked out of, as if all were his neighbors.

Cesar's magnetism was his sincerity.

We have heard of the numerous self-appointed leaders, supposed advocates for farmworkers, many of them ex-staff members of the union who deluded themselves that they could ride on Cesar's coattails and take over the leadership of this captive, meek group. They were to learn that insincerity comes with a tremendous putrid body odor. It can be sensed. The meek can smell insincerity the minute it walks in the door. Pseudo leaders were short-lived.

I was one of the volunteers. I assisted in the organizing of the workers in the Fresno area, but I truly do not think of it as organizing. These workers had already made up their minds. They just needed help in getting those authorization cards filled out and their name on a membership card. They, too, were drawn to Cesar.

Later I was a $5.00 a week staffer. I assisted in the grape boycott in Philadelphia. The consumers in the East received Chavez with the same warmth that the farmworkers did here in the West. They called themselves "The Friends of the Farmworkers." The farmworker has no idea of the tremendous support he or she has across the country. Cesar made the farmworkers' struggles into the people's cause.

The last time I spoke to Cesar was in La Paz, the farmworkers' headquarters. Jessie De La Cruz and I had gone there to attend one of the numerous reunions.

During the lunch break, we caught Cesar at one of those rare moments when he was not talking to a farmworker. Jessie wanted to take Cesar's picture. I said, "Cesar, all these

Profiles of power lift our struggles.

years we've known each other and I've never had my picture taken with you." He looked surprised that this was the case, and he agreed to pose with me.

Jessie was having trouble getting the camera to work. While she was fiddling with the film, I turned to Cesar, "You look tired. Are you feeling all right?"

"I haven't been feeling very well lately," he said. He started to say something else, but just then a group of members came over and surrounded him. Cesar turned and directed his attention to their concerns. Jessie and I moved away. That picture never happened.

Hope Lopez is currently writing her memoir of her years as a volunteer with the UFW.

Off the streets and on the road to respect.

There are many things that were impressive about Cesar Chavez. Certainly one of them was the tremendous compassion he felt for people who were exploited and the way in which he organized farmworkers professionally over a long span of years.

But the most impressive thing about Cesar was the way he allowed himself to grow spiritually as he worked with some of the poorest people in the country. Many professionals adopt a professional demeanor and stick with it. It becomes a protective shell and their way of coping. The shell keeps them at a distance from people. Cesar never assumed this posture.

Cesar allowed himself to be touched deeply by his spiritual beliefs and by the personal plight of the people and their personal hardships and suffering. By his belief in the transcendental dimensions of justice, he actually became a person very much in spiritual peace. And he intellectually understood the doctrines of nonviolence, of Ghandi-esque protests that led him to hunger strikes and boycotts and marches. But beyond intellect one simply had to look at his face to see an inner calm that came from knowing the rightness of his cause. He seemed to derive his power from the people, not himself.

In his classic study on leadership, James Magregor Burns talks about two kinds of leadership. One is transactional leadership in which leaders provide leadership in exchange for delivering results for clients or followers. Then Burns describes the transformational leader who transforms those around him by drawing on a higher power, such as a vision, a dream, a cause, a sense of justice.

There's no doubt between those types of leadership which kind of leader Cesar Chavez was. He was clearly a transforming leader who brought people together and inspired them to a new sense of themselves. As such, he didn't have to use the traditional instruments of leadership—exhortation, passionate speech, coercion, manipulation.

Quite the contrary, he relied on humility and a quiet calm to draw respect. Cesar aligned himself with the touchstone allegiances of the people: their church, Our Lady of Guadalupe, their working groups, the humility of their dress, their humble lifestyles, their understated speech, a certain purity of demeanor.

Even while aligned with the people, he was able to transform them and raise their awareness of the cause. The cause was to demand justice for people who were treated unfairly, whose wages were denied them, whose living quarters were inadequate. People were intimidated. Cesar was there for them.

Henry Cisneros is the president and CEO of Univision.

The time was the late 1960s and it was an announcement in the local newspaper that brought me to a small Methodist church in Huntington Beach, California to hear Cesar speak. We were about ten people and gathered in a circle with Cesar. Most of us were meeting him for the first time.

Cesar's message that evening was simple and straight forward. Farmworkers were in the midst of their first grape strike. "They need your help. This is what you can do. They need food, money for strikers, clergy and lay people on picket lines and support for economic boycotts. Even if people cannot give food or money, they can contribute by not buying certain products. For farmworkers, the boycott is the last nonviolent alternative."

Until that evening with Cesar, my plans were to return to public health nursing. But I'm reminded of Dolores Huerta who decided that she could accomplish more by organizing farmworkers than trying to teach their children who came to school hungry and without shoes. I didn't return to public health nursing.

Since that time I have worked as volunteer coordinator for the Orange County Interfaith Committee to Aid Farmworkers, the oldest support group for farmworkers in the United States established by Ralph Kennedy in 1965. I have also served on the executive committee of the National Farmworker Ministry and have been a member of the board for twenty-two years. My life—forever changed!

Jeanne Giordano is a registered nurse.

Marching into our future.

At some of the early union meetings, I recall a speech in which Cesar would say something like, "It is true you have awful wages and poor living and working conditions on these farms and ranches. It is your fault. You let them do it to you. And only you can change what is happening to you. You—we—have that power. Each of us has the power to control our lives. When we take that power, we can improve our living and working conditions."

During the planning stages of the first march to Sacramento in 1966, about fifteen of us went with Cesar to meet quietly on the beach at Carpenteria in the home of a union supporter. During one break in the planning sessions, we all went down to play on the beach. It was foggy and cold. We all wore jackets or sweaters. Cesar had a long silk scarf around his neck which flowed behind him as we ran up and down the beach. Tourists watched us with questioning eyes. One finally came up to me and asked if Cesar was an Italian director and if we were his entourage. I laughed and said, "No." But later, I realized the tourist wasn't far off the mark.

In the early days of the grape strike, in late 1965, there would be some partying on Saturday nights. On one of those nights as the party wore on, Cesar leaned over to Helen and said, "Let's go home and make another one."

For me, the essence of Cesar's life and the United Farm Workers Union is in the faces of the marchers shown in the photo used on this book's dust jacket—particularly the two women in the foreground. Cesar, through the union, gave farmworkers license to claim and exclaim their human dignity and the essential value of their work and lives.

George Elfie Ballis has been doing stills and movies on the edges of social change with farmworkers, civil rights organizers, working people and environmentalists for almost half a century.

I don't owe any money. I am a free man.

"De Colores"

I first met Cesar Chavez when I was twelve years old in 1962. My parents had become involved in the farmworker movement and my sisters and I were dragged from home to home as they moved from city to city to organize other farmworkers. I had no idea who this person was, why my parents followed him or the reasons behind the insanity that was created whenever Cesar Chavez was in my community. I remembered events that occurred during those early years of my youth when my sisters and I would rebel against my parents and their efforts to educate us against the injustices that we suffered as farmworkers. As the years went by, I began to understand what my parents and Cesar Chavez were trying to accomplish, not only for themselves but for their children and future generations.

In 1971, I decided to spend my summer vacation volunteering with the United Farm Workers Union. I took up its offer to volunteer for six weeks and I ended up staying for almost six years. During those years, I participated in many picket lines, landed in jail countless times, boycotted numerous businesses, lived in many different cities and states, and lectured in universities and at union meetings.

In 1973 Cesar decided that I was ready to run a boycott office in Sacramento. I moved to Sacramento and began setting up for this office. I rented space in a church, organized the students from California State University, Sacramento to picket Safeway stores, opened a checking account and rented a small place for myself. I did all that was required of me, but I made mistakes and the interest of the community and the students began to die down after six months. I was told to close up the office and to return to La Paz. I dreaded facing Cesar. I was terrified and afraid.

Many have said that Cesar was a kind and gentle man who understood that we all make mistakes in life. I made many mistakes in trying to run the Sacramento boycott office and Cesar understood that. I remember being in his office in La Paz (terrified, afraid, ashamed) and Cesar asking me what had gone wrong in Sacramento. I couldn't lie to him when his soft, gentle eyes encouraged me to tell the truth. He didn't let me belittle myself. He understood that I was too young and ignorant to handle a boycott office by myself. He made me feel proud that I had attempted to work out all the problems by myself. He gave me confidence that I could do anything I set my mind to do. He gave me trust and honesty and self-respect. These are traits that I admired in him. Traits that I pass on to my students and someday they will pass on to their children.

Elizabeth Hernandez worked the fields alongside her parents, brothers and sisters until 1971 and with the United Farm Workers Union from 1971 to 1976. She received her bachelor of arts degree with a credential in bilingual education from Fresno State University in 1980.

Cesar's first long fast was during the Vietnam War. I was privileged to be there when he broke the fast, in the presence of Bobby Kennedy and such other notables as Walter Reuther, head of the AFL-CIO. We were all left with a great impression of the power of fasting.

The following Lent, a few of us, led by Chris Hartmire, who was at that time head of the California Migrant Ministry, decided to have a fast for Holy Week focusing on our opposition to the war. We would meet in a church in downtown Los Angeles each day during the noon hour for mutual support. Cesar heard about the fast from Chris. He knew it was a very small group. Cesar's health had not fully recovered from his own fast and it was difficult for him to ride in a car for long distances but he came down to Los Angeles to be with us and offer his support.

During the time of sharing he told us, in a very humble way, what the fast meant to him. He said this was an opportunity for him to explore before God his own motivations in the movement and to be very clear that this was God's doing. He was determined that he and the movement remain true to nonviolence. He knew that many did not understand this fast and that some would be driven away. But he knew his people would stay with him. Many people later reflected that the fast was a great strategy for calling attention to the strike, but those who heard him that day knew of his deeper stirrings.

In the mid-60s, as the campaign reached a national level, Cesar went on a trip around the country promoting the grape boycott. I was privileged to be present at a gathering when Cesar returned. He spoke with enthusiasm of the many he met around the country who were working on the boycott. But he said he was also very impressed with the many dedicated persons he met working on other causes, such as prison reform. After hearing of the suffering and the struggle of other poor people, he declared that we must not only champion *La Raza* but *La Raza Humana*. Cesar's sense of solidarity only grew from that point on.

All of us were deeply shocked when we heard of the death of Martin Luther King. One of my Franciscan brothers told me that Cesar wanted to have a prayer service to honor the loss of this great leader of nonviolence. Many were concerned that since Cesar was also a well-known leader of a nonviolent poor people's movement he might also be a target for such a vicious attack.

Cesar had received death threats. He was cautioned to lie low during this time. But instead, he called for the gathering and was present in the hall. He spoke of the closeness he felt to Martin and his respect for the commitment of Martin to nonviolence. He was very touched by the loss of the great leader and pledged himself to carry on the struggle for the people and nonviolence.

During the mid-80s the Franciscans held a conference in Oakland focusing on nonviolence. Cesar came and spoke with us. During a question period after his talk, a young women who was a strong animal rights advocate spoke up to say that many did not know that Cesar was a vegetarian. Although I had quite a bit of exposure to Cesar, I was quite surprised to hear this. Cesar then responded that he had taken this commitment because it did not seem consistent to him to be for nonviolence and to kill and eat animals. That was more than fifteen years ago and I have never been able to eat meat again since that day.

Louis Vitale is a Franciscan friar from the St. Boniface Community in San Francisco, California.

I recall Cesar once comparing the art of organizing to harvesting grapes. When he first saw the vines stretching to the horizon, he wondered how he could ever accomplish such a task. "By concentrating on one bunch at a time," he said. Cutting each as he reached it, eventually the entire vineyard would be harvested.

Jacques Levy is the author of Cesar Chavez: Autobiography of La Causa.

I'm paid pennies a pound for picking peas. It's not a living, but I eat some.

MARIA RIFO

To me Cesar Chavez was a visionary for his people and many others. As a child, he suffered the injustice of the ranchers and people with power. Because of that experience, he could transmit his ideals of justice to his people, the farmworkers. They understood what he wanted for them and followed him without reserve. Not only the farmworkers were touched by his philosophy, but also many volunteers and people with power.

In my case, as a volunteer, he changed my life's perspective 180 degrees. He made me discover all that I am now, which had been submerged due to lack of incentive. The same happened to hundreds of people who had the fortune to be touched by him and his visionary spirit. He knew how to listen. He was patient with those he saw could give something back. He gave them time.

Originally a teacher from Chile, Maria Rifo came to work at La Paz as Cesar's personal secretary.

We have a right to the fruits of this life.

Cesar was my brother back in the 1940s. He lived near us. One day when I was five or seven years old, Cesar asked me, "Do you know when I'm going to see you again?"

As a kid it was very confusing to understand that even though you were in America, you were not an American. People called you Mexican. My mother was Portuguese so other people would call me Portuguese. So I never knew what was going on. What are we? Mexicans, Americans or Portuguese?

When Cesar came into our lives next, it was the early 1960s. Everybody needed a leader and he came at the perfect time. People were members of other groups but Cesar started the UFW and three-quarters of the people automatically moved over.

Sometimes he would just come over to our house. He would ask what our conditions were, did we need better wages, things like that. He would go from house to house.

We got into the union with the September 8 strike of 1965. I remember talking about the strike as good for the welfare of everybody. The strike benefited every worker, all men and women that are in the field. The conditions were really bad. No toilets in the fields, no drinking cold water. If you asked for a raise, you were laid off. The crew was about half Mexicans and half Filipinos. They said this is our ranch and we'll do what we want. If you don't like it, you can go. That was the attitude.

My whole family came out for the strike. I quit my job because of the strike. The whole family was there. My mom was sixty-three years old.

We used to work really late in San Francisco. On top of this we needed money, food and clothing. This is how it was the first few months of the strike. But we knew that the boycott was necessary to win.

Once I was in a camp that got up at 4:00 A.M. and went to strike at 6:00 A.M. There was a policeman there asking me what right we had to wake people up. We said we had every right because there's a strike on.

I would carry around in my wallet a copy of the Constitution and a Supreme Court ruling on picketing. I challenged the police with it. Sometime they got a little arrogant. I'd say, "Here, read what it says here. You are violating my rights." They'd look at that like they couldn't believe it. I would tell them it was a Supreme Court ruling. It caught their eye. I often had to challenge several police before going on my way picketing.

I think when Cesar came there wasn't much for a young Chicano. At the time it was really difficult to understand what the hell was going on. We looked up to actors like Anthony Quinn or Ricardo Monteban as role models. In my mind somebody would someday come along and do something for a Chicano. I would follow that person.

To me, it was the man. I had a lot of respect for him. A lot of love for him. He came into our lives when we really needed him. I think he wanted us to feel worthwhile.

In Delano and everywhere, Cesar would say the labor contractors had a right to hire and fire, but not to steal and they had done a lot of stealing. These were people pretending to be leaders of the people, pretending to lead them to better working conditions and wages. You'd pay them a certain fee and they'd stick it in their pocket. That happened a lot. The distrust was very deep among the workers. When Cesar came he put no demands on the workers.

He would ask the people, "What do you think should be the wage here in the Valley and throughout California?"

I went back to New York for Cesar and the union in 1965. I was a boycotter, farmworker on strike, whatever you called it.

One thing Cesar showed us was to love the person who hates you.

Being a Chicano from Delano, you have to know when to stand up for your rights, then here comes a man who tells you you have to be nonviolent.

Cesar would say to me, "We go a long way back, but if you can't accept nonviolence, then just leave." It hurt, but I

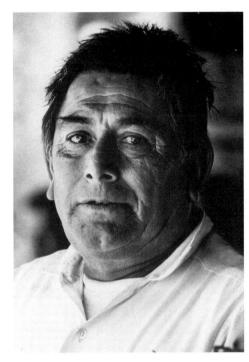

Every road I've traveled is a line in my face.

Everybody did their part. The thing I remember most in respect of Cesar is that he would never tell a person to do something that he wasn't doing himself. Rain or shine, bright or snow, he was there. We considered it a war.

The growers stick together. Cesar told us that you cannot win without organizing. You have to organize the people at the ranch. They have to organize their own ranch. You reap only what you put in. You never decline anyone's help. If they told you maybe, then you would ask them when they were ready to change that to a yes.

We would use whatever nonviolent tactic it took. A lady from the Rockettes remarked that she gave money to various causes. She said she had trouble deciding which causes to give to. She said our organization was fourth or fifth on her list. I told her we needed that money more than anyone else and that I'd have Cesar come and tell her how the money would be used. I had it arranged. Six months later she put us on the top of her list. She gave us $5000.

Manuel Vasquez is a farmworker and activist.

understood because he told me that every farm labor group that had been in power ended up in violence—but those groups aren't around anymore.

I was upset. But I learned that this was true. We wouldn't be in existence right now if it wasn't for nonviolence. This is the difference between violence and nonviolence. When you organize someone with your fists, you've only organized them as long as you have your fist in their face. But if you organize with nonviolence in light of the true facts, that they're being exploited, that their conditions can be changed, then you can work together. Then it is everlasting.

We had a meeting in Delano. Cesar asked for volunteers to go to the East. In 1968 they left a skeleton crew back in Delano. It took us about ten stops to go across the country. Every night we slept in buildings. In 1973 I was sent to Los Angeles.

The union is a creation of the people. You feel great.

*Dolores Huerta, cofounder
of the UFW, calls to field workers to join La Causa.*

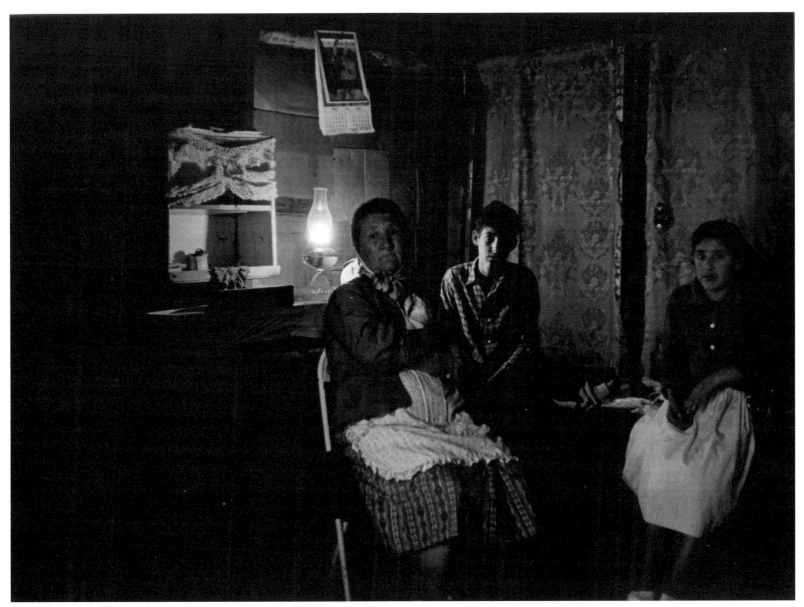

We need more than one kerosene lamp to bring us into the light.

Cesar Chavez was a man not unlike most other men. He did not come from a privileged background. He didn't even have a high school diploma. His life was—by most Mexican-American standards of his day—pretty normal. Cesar, along with many of us, suffered the harsh realities of a life of farm work which brings with it a life of extreme poverty and discrimination. He was, by most definitions, a common man.

But like many dreamers who came before him, Cesar was a common man who did uncommon things.

The United Farm Workers and the movement it created changed the lives of many thousands of farmworkers and touched the lives of countless others. Both supporters and opposition alike—from growers to workers, politicians to celebrities, students to professors, union leaders to religious leaders, police to strikers and millions of supporters and friends—came away touched by the sheer radiance and commitment Cesar projected. This determination that altered the lives of so many, created a whirlwind of social change and social justice. It has created strong leaders in the farmworker movement. Many who cut their teeth organizing for the UFW went on to lead the way through a myriad of political issues.

But what was it about Cesar that made him the extraordinary person he was? Many would say it was his charisma. Others might speak of his sheer will. I believe it was simply his humanity that made him stand out from the rest of us. Because, you see, Cesar Chavez was a contradiction. While he stood out from a crowd, he also was one of them, and no better a person than any of us have the power to be. His difference—I believe—was that he utilized this power.

I first met Cesar in 1968 in Denver, Colorado when he and several busloads of workers came on one of the stops on the historic pilgrimage of the first grape boycott. I remember standing in a hall packed with members of the local labor movement, students, Chicano activists and many, many others. I watched as these farmworkers climbed off the bus and filed into the hall. I was struck by how humble they all looked, not unlike my mother and father—like my aunts and uncles, who themselves were all migrant farmworkers—like me, who grew up working in the fields.

They were led into the hall by a small, soft-spoken man who did not brandish the bravado or the verbosity of so many other leaders and historic figures of the time. Little did I know that not too long after, I would be working for this man and it would forever influence my approach to organizing, to life, to love and all that sits in between.

From 1969 to 1974 Magdaleno worked as a UFW staff member. In 1994 he returned to La Paz as the executive director of the Cesar E. Chavez Foundation.

When I was young, Cesar's family and my family went up to the snow. My brother had this big aluminum Coca Cola cap. My brother and I were supposed to get on it and slide down so we climbed up the mountain. I got on it first and I guess I slipped out of my brother's hand and I went down the mountain by myself. I was screaming to my mom because I got scared. I had my eyes closed. My mom got scared. Between Cesar and my dad they were trying to stop me and they finally did stop me at the bottom of the hill. Cesar was making fun of me.

Afterwards when I got older, I forgot all about this until we moved to Delano and I was going to school there. Every time Cesar would see me he'd say, "Remember the trip to the mountains? Do you want to go to the mountains? To the snow again?" I'd just laugh and tell him no.

When I started working for him in the office, the first thing he'd do when introducing me to someone was to tell them what happened that year up at the mountains. He'd just laugh and smile at me and say, "Do you still want to go up to the snow?"

That's something I always remember about him. He'd always make me laugh.

Now that he's gone I find it really hard. I remember when I found out he passed away, I couldn't believe it. This man has passed away. This man I'd known for so long. I looked up to him as a father and a friend—someone who you could go up to and say, "I have a problem. Can I talk to you for a minute?" It never mattered how busy he was; he would always have time for you. If he didn't have time, he would make it while you were there waiting for him—even if he was going to a meeting or something. I remember going up to him and saying, "I have a problem, Cesar. I need to talk to you." He said, "OK. Give me a minute. Wait for me at my office."

I went to his office and waited for him. He walked in a few minutes later and said, "C'mon, let's go outside for a walk. It's a pretty morning. So we went out the back door to Forty Acres. We just went outside and walked around talking. I was telling him my problems and he just listened to me. He didn't judge me. He listened and said, "Well, there's some things I can tell you and there's some things I can't. Some things are up to you."

He was the type of person that if you wanted to talk to him about something he'd listen but that was as far as it was going to go. Nobody else was ever going to know about this problem unless you told them. He never would.

He asked me what I wanted to do about it and I told him, and he said, "OK. If that's what you want, then that's what we'll do."

He was very gentle. He always went out of his way to say hello to you if he knew you. I thought it was fun to be around him. I used to love to hear him talk. At times he was funny; he'd make you laugh. Other times it was business only. I don't ever remember him raising his voice to anyone. If he ever got mad, you could hardly tell. He was cool and calm. He would listen. He was very understanding. There were times I thought he had the patience of a saint.

He was always there to lend a helping hand if he could. When my mother passed away, I remember he helped us out then too. I think the worst thing about that was I never got a chance to thank him for it. I always kept saying I was going to go see him and thank him. I thought he'd live forever.

Carmen Hernandez is a friend of the Chavez family.

—

From many places, down many roads, we manifest a multitude.

¡Viva La Huelga!

I remember Cesar as so fiercely devoted to farmworker rights as to be unforgiving of whoever or whatever undermined his struggle to set them free. I remember him as having enormous trust in a person's ability to do a task or to learn how to do it. I did many things in my nearly three and a half years of volunteer service that I had never done before. I also remember Cesar as humble and very human. Though a vegetarian, he enjoyed seeing his coworkers relish a pig roast, albeit with a bit of teasing!

When I was working at union headquarters in La Paz, he came to my room, along with his two dogs, Huelga and Boycott, to talk about my work in the School of Negotiations. I don't recall what we talked about, but I am still impressed that he took time to come to see me and to listen. I joined in one of his long marches across California and attended to his needs on one of his fasts. In both instances he was always very grateful and never denied his pain and suffering. Cesar had an unrelenting drive—we all worked six-day weeks and ten-hour days, that is, when things were normal—and there was never any doubt that the well-being of farmworkers always came first.

Sister Betty Wolcott is a Sister of St. Francis of Assisi. For three years, Sister Betty experienced the plight of migrant farmworkers as a volunteer for the United Farm Workers in California.

*When Cesar leaves,
I carry his spirit onward.*

"Once people understand the strength of
nonviolence, the force it generates, the love it
creates, the response it brings from the total
community, they will not easily abandon it."
—Cesar Chavez

I first met Cesar Chavez in the early 1970s, and I have many warm memories of the time I was able to spend with him. I had a clear understanding from the beginning of our relationship that he was a rare and special kind of leader, completely devoid of ego, uninterested in the limelight and devoted to the cause of oppressed farmworkers. In 1974, I presented The King Center's highest award, the Martin Luther King, Jr. Nonviolent Peace Prize, to him in recognition of his uncompromising dedication to nonviolent social change in the spirit of Martin's teachings.

We proudly supported Cesar and the UFW during their organizing campaigns in California and Florida and their boycotts of lettuce and grapes. I marched with Cesar and his followers in California, New York and Atlanta.

When I visited his office in La Paz, I was struck by the simplicity of the surroundings and how humble the material resources were.

Cesar considered himself a disciple of Martin, just as my husband was a disciple of Gandhi. Cesar told me that the United Farm Workers modeled many of their campaigns on the nonviolent principles and strategies we employed in the Civil Rights Movement.

On another occasion, I was invited to deliver the keynote address at a rally in front of the jail in Salinas, where Cesar was incarcerated for civil disobedience in a protest for better wages and working conditions for the farmworkers. I remember that a priest read from Martin's writings at the Salinas rally. I also visited Cesar in Arizona during one of his many fasts for justice for the farmworkers. Although he was weak from fasting, he sat through a press conference and rally.

Cesar embodied a powerful humility and a great sense of dignity and decency. He had such a gentle spirit, quiet courage and radiant integrity, I always left our meeting feeling renewed and inspired.

Coretta Scott King is the founder of The Martin Luther King, Jr. Center for Nonviolent Social Change.

I am Aztec-Christian.

Child, hear my heart
beat for your possibilities.

The first of my two personal encounters with Cesar took place on August 2, 1973, at the industrial farm in Caruthers, California where I was incarcerated along with 400 strikers. On July 30, I had driven to Fresno with three United Farm Workers supporters from Santa Clara County to stay overnight. At dawn on the thirty-first, we drove to Parlier and joined a group that included several busloads of priests and nuns from all over the United States who volunteered to be arrested in defiance of an anti-picketing ordinance. The purpose was to bring publicity to the union which was fighting for its life against the incursion of the Teamsters. In what seemed to be a preplanned scenario, we walked for three-quarters of an hour carrying signs on a road outside a nectarine ranch, after which we were picked up by the county sheriff's department buses and taken to the Caruthers honor farm for a ten-day stay. It was a totally peaceful operation.

That summer, as the Watergate hearings were revealing the sleaze in Washington, Caruthers was the place to be. We were visited by celebrities including Daniel Ellsberg, who had incurred Nixon's wrath by leaking the Pentagon papers to *The New York Times*. Joan Baez arrived with him and sang one of the year's top ten hits to the amazement of the regular prisoners. Dorothy Day of *Catholic Worker* fame was with us enjoying what she said was the most comfortable of a long series of jail experiences which began with the women's suffrage protests before the First World War. There was a relaxed atmosphere at Caruthers. With the presence of Dorothy Day and the priests and nuns—and the influence of the Catholic church staff and protesters, both farmworkers and lay people—it was like a summer camp with political and religious overtones.

On the day that Cesar Chavez came into our large, airy dormitory and greeted us one by one, he shook my hand and said, "Thank you for coming, Sister." Although I was pleased to be mistaken for one of those remarkable women I had grown to admire, I answered, "Oh, but I'm not a Sister." Whereupon he gave a response that I have repeated many times to family and friends; he said, "You are a Sister."

My second and very different meeting with Cesar took place several years later on a picket line outside a supermarket in San Jose, California. In the intervening time I had done research on farm labor leaders in the 1930s who belonged to a Communist Party union and were tried and convicted and sent to state prison under a criminal syndicalism law that was then in effect in California. Cesar told me that one of these leaders, Pat Chambers, the chief organizer of the 1933 San Joaquin Valley cotton pickers' strike, had visited La Paz. I had heard Ernesto Galarza, a leader of the National Farm Labor Union in the late 1940s and early 1950s, mention Chambers and his associates in a speech to a group of UFW supporters. Galarza said that the experiences of these individuals with the vigilante tactics of growers (as documented by the LaFollette Committee of the U.S. Senate in 1940) had made organizing less perilous for later generations of farm labor leaders. I was impressed that both Chavez and Galarza—who despite impeccable credentials had themselves been subjected to red-baiting—readily acknowledged the historical legacy of an outlawed union.

Anne Loftis is the coauthor of A Long Time Coming: The Struggle to Unionize America's Farm Workers *and* Witness to the Struggle: Imaging the 1930s California Labor Movement.

When I went to Helen Chavez at Cesar's funeral to offer my love and sympathy, she said, "Paul, I have my memories." Helen is special, was Cesar's full-time partner and has more memories than any of us.

My earliest memory of Cesar in action was on December 16, 1965, when we had arranged for Walter Reuther, president of my union, the United Auto Workers, to visit Delano and to offer support for the three-month-old grape strike.

We had arranged for national media to join us to expose the plight of the farmworkers so that their isolated efforts to build a union would get national attention and support. In isolation, strikers became the targets of the violence of certain growers, their goons and their sheriffs.

It became obvious to us through that exciting day and night that Cesar was indeed a natural leader who was as gentle as he was strong and who had the patience to carry on the struggle for justice. We decided to give full support to that struggle and to Cesar via long-term financial contributions and strategic support.

I remember that on this occasion Cesar said, "Walter gives me confidence." And Cesar's confidence gave farmworkers confidence to organize and fight. We felt his deep commitment to the cause of the farmworkers and their families. He knew the difficulties he faced, particularly the near total economic and political power of the big growers and·the vulnerability of the farmworkers to this power.

Three months after the Reuther visit, we asked Robert Kennedy to come to investigate farmworker problems. He did come in March of 1966 with the U.S. Senate Migratory Workers Committee. In those three days in the San Joaquin Valley, Kennedy discovered and exposed to the public the terrible living and working conditions of farmworker families. That convinced him to join the struggle just as he had the civil rights struggle after investigating similar conditions in Mississippi.

I define my life.

I remember the public hearing in Delano High School, Cesar's first-ever testimony before a Senate committee. He was impressive in his sincerity and thoughtfulness as he challenged the illegal strike-breaking of the growers and the need for legislation. Kennedy picked up on those issues and challenged the illegal mass arrests of peaceful pickets by Sheriff Galyen of Kern County and instructed him to read the U.S. Constitution during lunch break.

Later that day Kennedy endorsed the grape strike and boycott at a farmworker rally at Filipino Hall and walked the mile-long picket line at the DiGiorgio ranch. No other national politician had ever done this. Kennedy showed that he cared and he acted.

Robert Kennedy and his family joined the boycott, helped raise funds and tried to influence government on behalf of farmworkers. Nothing was heard from other national public leaders despite requests. Vice President Hubert Humphrey on behalf of President Johnson asked Bert Corona for Latino support in the 1968 elections. Bert told him that he would have to support the farmworker struggle. Humphrey replied, "We can't do that."

We invited Robert Kennedy to come back to Delano on March 10, 1968, to celebrate the end of Cesar's long fast against violence. He was the only political leader invited to that huge rally. Again, he came. Cesar, extremely weak and extremely sick, asked him to run for president. Days later Kennedy announced that he would.

We began organizing a slate of delegates to the Democratic National Convention in support of Kennedy. Cesar was invited to join the delegation but had not decided. I remember his concern was that if he did, he might lose important support from AFL-CIO president George Meany who was supporting President Johnson for reelection.

On March 19, I was challenged by UAW President Reuther at our national board meeting because of my public endorsement of Kennedy. That night I called Kennedy at home. He had agreed to call Cesar and make a personal request to join the delegation.

I asked him about that. He said, "Cesar sounded so sick and so weak from the fast, I didn't have the heart to ask him to do it." He knew that Cesar would risk losing the support of Meany.

I replied to Kennedy, "That doesn't sound like the cold-blooded, ruthless S.O.B. you are supposed to be." He chuckled and asked me not to tell anyone.

I called Cesar and told him of my talk with Kennedy and discussed my problem with Reuther and his with Meany. He said he would call a membership meeting. Within hours several hundred UFW members met in Delano and unanimously instructed him to join the Kennedy delegation. I then agreed to join the delegation. Cesar had given me confidence.

Cesar knew that Robert Kennedy was the only presidential candidate committed to the farmworkers struggle. Cesar knew that he had to do what was best for the members of his union. That took great strength and courage to confront major supporters like Meany and Reuther and support Kennedy.

I remembered that we agreed that Kennedy was the only presidential candidate who could and would end the war against the people of Vietnam and support the cause of the farmworkers. Cesar, who strongly opposed all violence, was horrified by this terrible war that was forcing American workers and their sons to kill peasants in a distant land and to die there without cause.

Kennedy won in California because the farmworkers union registered tens of thousands of new voters and turned them out to vote on June 4, 1968. Their rural and urban community action in support of the grape strike and boycott paid off in the election with the greatest turnout in the barrios and ghettos ever.

Then violence took Kennedy from us. And we all lost.

My lasting memory is Cesar's strength and courage, his gentleness and his determination to win justice and dignity for all. He gave us all confidence and hope of victory on this long march to justice. And I loved the marches, the music and the red banners flying. I still do. We must continue.

Viva *La Causa*! Viva *Solidaridad*! Viva Cesar Chavez!

Paul Schrade was western director of the United Auto Workers union when he organized support for the farmworkers struggle in 1965.

Long row.
Long road.

A thing that I remember about Cesar was his thirst for knowledge. He wanted to know everything he could about any topic he dealt with. And he wanted those around him to know as much as they could.

In 1971, I worked for a year on security at La Paz. This included working at times with Cesar's well-trained dogs, Boycott and Huelga. Cesar loaned me a book about training dogs. He told me that since security required him to have dogs, he chose to make a hobby of that necessity.

About 1977, Cesar decided that we needed to upgrade our management skills at La Paz. We had a three-day seminar on management. A list of topics was put together. Then each of us chose one of the topics to research and report on it to the rest of the staff. In addition, Cesar gave all of us a book to read. I think the title was *Management by Objectives*.

About 1978, we began some educational programs, including language courses—English for the farmworkers, Spanish for the Anglo volunteers. At that time Cesar had been reading about the Lozanov method of education and liked what he read about it. We got Dr. Georgi Lozanov's book and read it. We incorporated his methodology into the language program as well as some other ideas that Cesar had about language learning.

Patrick Bonner worked fulltime with the union from 1968 to 1973. He spent three years in Los Angeles, one year in La Paz and one year in Phoenix. He returned in 1976 for the Proposition 14 campaign, then spent most of the next four years in La Paz.

*The earth and I
are of one mind,
one heart, one spirit, one body.*

Cesar Chavez shared so much of himself and the struggle of the farmworkers with Delancey Street that we've always felt our two extended families are joined as one.

We often served as Cesar's bodyguards. Perfect for us at Delancey Street because we allow no violence. When we joined Cesar in the marches and meetings, we somehow felt our ex-felon status offered him special protection. Certainly his presence always offered us a special protection from ever getting too compliant.

There were two events that Cesar and I shared at Delancey Street every year from 1974 until he died: the annual Delancey dinner held on September 16 and a late March, dual celebration of our birthdays—his was March 31 and mine March 29.

Cesar would often come to our Delancey dinner several days early to help our residents research the history and prepare the dances of their heritage. At every September 16 dinner, he would get up in his cardigan and talk about Father Hidalgo. As he told the story, he would move into the struggle of both Delancey Street and the farmworkers and talk about what it felt like to be a small band of people who felt helpless and poor, but with the courage to find a way to fight for their freedom. He never spoke angrily, nor did he ever try to rouse the crowd. He simply spoke from his heart. At the end of every September 16 dinner, 500 former ex-felons always rose to their feet, many unashamedly had tears falling down their cheeks, all cheering "Viva! Viva! Viva!" His basic truth and commitment to all of us who felt so left out of the American dream broke through all of the biases, anger and despair, year after year.

Our birthday celebrations held the same tone. Sometimes our dinners were simple with John Maher and me and Helen and my twin boys David and Greg—who in their young years could never understand why Cesar would have a special party where he could eat any food he wanted and would only eat vegetables, and, in later years could not

My soul hungers for justice.

understand how the country could still ignore the pleas Cesar was making against pesticides and other injustices. Often Jimmy Herman, the head of the International Longshoremen and Warehousemen's Union, would join us and we'd all share dreams about how things were going to be different next year.

Our birthdays also coincide with Delancey Street's, and I especially remember when Delancey decided to celebrate its tenth anniversary with a very fancy black-tie dinner, with all kinds of Hollywood stars and society folks dressed in glittering clothes. After endless luminaries and statesmen gave us commendations and awards and glowing speeches, it was Cesar's turn to speak. He came to the podium in his same cardigan and, as he did at every talk, he addressed his remarks not to the suits and ties and guests in the room, but to the newest Delancey Street residents. He talked of their struggles, of how hard it is to believe and hope that things could be different, to believe that they themselves could change, to believe that there would be real opportunities for them as they rebuilt their lives. He talked of his struggles and ours as one. And, as always, he reached the heart.

The false "big-shotitis" that might have taken us over for a moment quickly faded as the man in the cardigan reminded us of what our birthdays meant and what they would always mean—a new beginning for decency and justice for all of the people left out and tossed out. Happy birthday, Cesar. Viva the dreams and viva the struggles to make them happen. I promise never to get complacent.

Mimi Silbert is president and CEO of the Delancey Street Foundation.

Look up at my spirit, not down on my poverty.

"One thing you must remember is that people, no matter how poor, how disadvantaged, still have the same aspirations as you do, for their children, for the future."

—Cesar Chavez

My memories of Cesar have been deep and dear from the moment Nan Cindy was taken from us at the Talisman Sugar picket line in Belle Glade, Florida. His concern and heartfelt warmth were a great comfort to my wife Selma and me at a time when words could not relieve the pain.

I remember the time when Cesar briefly visited our home in Wakefield, Massachusetts, in between his strenuous schedule of activity. We hoped that the short rest or quick dip in the pool would refresh his boundless energy.

I also remember the time when we joined Cesar at lunch at the farmworkers' home in Dorchester, Massachusetts. He invited me to try a taste of the hot peppers they served. A tiny piece could cure any and all ailments. It was probably the key to his unlimited drive.

Milton Freeman was the father of Nan Cindy Freeman, an 18 year old college student who, in 1972, was knocked down and killed by a tractor-trailer while helping to pass out leaflets during a 4:00 A.M. picket at Talisman Sugar Company near Belle Glade, Florida.

Facing the annual spring starving.

Into the fullness of my resolve.

I remember coming home after the 1966 march from Delano to Sacramento. We had a big station wagon with the Virgin Mary in the back.

The security people were devoted. It was hard. You go on the road. We would go to San Francisco and then they would say they needed you in Oakland or hours south in San Diego. I was the one who would go early in the morning with my 1952 Chevy and find the crews. We ran out of money. We were number one security for the man. It was forty-six hours a day. We would eat cookies, cheese and crackers.

When Cesar died, I didn't cry. I felt strange about that. I asked people why they thought I didn't cry. I still go by La Paz. No tears.

It was hard work working for the union, but it was fun. I believe I'm a better person today because of it. Cesar introduced me to people who turned my life around. Those were probably the best years of my life. It was exciting.

You can't be fearful. You have to always stand up for your rights.

I believe Cesar was sent to us by God. He stood up with no fear in his eyes. He made you feel like you could do anything. It gave you self-confidence. These are things I try to pass on to my kids.

Michael S. Vasquez was one of the few original peregrinos from the UFW's 1966 Delano to Sacramento march who also joined the union for its second trek along the same route in 1994. In addition to handling security for Cesar, Mike worked on the 1970 grape boycott in Connecticut, Chicago and New York.

Viva Bobby, Viva la victoria.

He had been a personal hero nearly all of my adult life and a powerful source of inspiration, yet I had never met Cesar Chavez. It was early August, 1988, in hot and dusty Delano and he was on the twentieth day of his "Fast for Love" hunger protest at the United Farm Workers' headquarters. After my son Emilio had urged me to get involved, I had made several trips from Los Angeles over the three previous weeks to offer support and attend the Mass held every evening just after sundown in the union hall.

In his weakening condition, these Masses were the only public appearances Cesar was able to make. Aided by family and friends, he would walk the 300 or so yards from his small room in a slow, methodical procession to the hall. The noisy, overflowing crowd of family, rank and file and supporters would fall to an instant hush as he appeared at the door and slowly moved to his place near the makeshift altar. It was in this setting that I had my first glimpse of him, which lives in the heart of my memory with fondness and awe.

Cesar's physical size alone was a stunning realization. I had always imagined him this giant figure striding through the San Joaquin Valley gathering all the farmworkers under his mantle and confronting all the growers with his mandate. For nearly a quarter of a century it seemed he soared like the UFW black eagle to the heights of our imaginations and captured our hearts with his boundless courage.

In fact, he was barely five foot tall with a shy, gentle manner and a disarming smile, but soon the reality of his being would become far more powerful than my long-held image of him.

Several days later I returned to Delano with my wife Janet to join our friends Father William O'Donnell, whom we affectionately call Bill and Dr. Davida Coady, who had driven down from Oakland to support "Fast for Love" and to hold vigil. Bill was an early supporter of the UFW from the 1960s and a longtime friend of Cesar's. It was the twenty-third day of the fast and Cesar's condition was rapidly deteriorating, causing widespread concern and, despite Bill's upbeat personality, he had become very worried. Then suddenly and very casually he asked Janet and me if we would like to meet Cesar. I had to catch my breath before I could respond.

"But that's impossible now with his condition and the circumstances," I said.

This response was prompted by the fact that I had heard that Cesar was so weak he could no longer receive visitors.

"Let me ask around and find out," Bill said. And off he went.

While I waited, I became nervous, contemplating the possibility, however remote, that I might actually meet Cesar Chavez very shortly! I was a heavy smoker at that time and the more I thought of this extraordinary opportunity, the more it fired my imagination and my smoking habit. By the time Bill returned, I was chain smoking.

"Come on," he said excitedly, "he wants to meet you."

Bill led the way toward Cesar's room.

"You know, I don't have any idea what to say to him," I said as we walked. Trying to cover my apprehension, I added, "I just didn't think this chance would come right now."

"Don't worry," Bill said reassuringly, "the meeting will be very brief. He's not feeling well but he wants to wish you a happy birthday."

I had just celebrated my forty-eighth birthday a few days earlier. When we reached the door I bid everyone go inside assuring them I'd be right along as soon as I had finished my cigarette. Bill and Davida agreed and went in but Janet stayed with me. Taking one long, last, deep drag I said with trepidation, "Imagine, he's just on the other side of that door!"

"Of course he is," Janet responded with annoyance, "Where else would he be? Now put that damn cigarette out and go in with me to meet him."

With that admonishment, I stepped on the cigarette, pulled open the door and followed Janet into the room. Once inside I took everything in as quickly as possible. The room

Our hopes ride on the crest of our voices.

was small and crowded with family members and union officials on one side, while Bill and Davida stood next to Cesar, who lay on a small, single bed against the wall near the only window. Observing Cesar laying down made him appear even smaller than I had glimpsed him three days earlier. As Janet proceeded me, and I heard the introduction, suddenly everything around me seemed suspended and I felt an overwhelming sense of calm to the depths of my being which brought tears of joy to my eyes. Cesar greeted Janet with a warm smile and extended his hand which she kissed. He then returned her extraordinary gesture with equal reverence. Janet moved aside and Bill introduced me. Again, Cesar extended his hand which I took in both of mine and kissed as Janet had done. He held on to my hand and repeated the gesture, kissing my hand as well.

I cannot quite remember what words may have passed between us because the instant he kissed my hand I became embarrassingly aware that my hand had held a cigarette only seconds earlier and it must have been revolting for him. When I was able to refocus my attention, someone had come forward with a small, red and black union flag and Cesar was signing it for me as a birthday gift. Very shortly afterwards we said our good-byes and departed.

Despite my embarrassment I nearly floated back to the union hall clutching the precious flag, and somewhere along the way I resolved that I would make some personal sacrifice to help support Cesar's "Fast for Love."

That resolve became a vow to myself that I would stop smoking for as long as Cesar fasted. Eleven days later at a special outdoor Mass, attended by thousands of supporters from all over the country, including Ethel Kennedy and Jesse Jackson, Cesar ended his fast after thirty-four long and pain-filled days. Immediately after the Mass I began to keep my no smoking vow and thirty-four days later I decided to extend it to one more day at a time.

Nearly five years later, I saw Cesar Chavez for the last time at a human rights function in downtown Los Angeles. Coincidentally, Bill and Dr. Coady were present as well. By then I had become an active UFW supporter and I was very proud that Cesar now counted me among his friends. We saw each other frequently at demonstrations, rallies and union gatherings in Los Angeles and La Paz. There was no reason to suspect that we would not continue to see each other often in the future. But it was not to be.

Several weeks later the news of his sudden death shook us all like a mighty earthquake. When I recovered from the shock, I reflected on our last conversation.

"Are you still not smoking?" Cesar asked.

"Yes sir," I replied proudly. "Thanks to you."

Thanks to him for all the countless other gifts as well.

Martin Sheen is an actor and ardent activist.

Acknowledgments

I wish to offer my sincere gratitude to all who shared their memories of Cesar Chavez for this book. I also wish to thank George Elfie Ballis whose photographs tell their own moving story and Cindy Wathen for her brilliant partnering.

Ann McGregor

I acknowledge the farmworkers who allowed me and my cameras into their lives so I could, with my photographs, reflect back to them their dignity, persistence and strength.

George Elfie Ballis

My admiration and gratitude to Ann and George for a lifetime of persistence in keeping Cesar's message alive. Thank you also to the many laborers, activists, supporters and contributors who took the time, often under difficult circumstances, to record their memories. Special thanks to Mary Ann Heron at the National Farm Worker Ministry for tirelessly answering my questions, to John Koontz for his unending support and to Bonnie Hearn, teacher, mentor and above all, friend.

Cindy Wathen

Permissions

Marc Grossman's essay (page 2) was excerpted from "By Giving Our Lives We Find Life" by Marc Grossman in Stone Soup for The World, *edited by Marianne Larned, copyright © 1998 by Marianne Larned, by permission of Conari Press.*